THE NEW CANADIAN RETIREMENT

An Action Plan to Construct
a Rock Solid Retirement

By Brian Mercer

ISBN: 1497405920
ISBN 13: 9781497405929

Dedication

To Becky, Carly, Cayley and Cullen,
for making the journey so worthwhile.

CONTENTS

CHAPTER ONE:

IS IT TIME YET?

Welcome to retirement, baby boomers

Every day, according to Statistics Canada, about one thousand Canadians turn sixty-five.

Retirees are becoming more abundant in our society as the "baby boom" generation ages. These baby boomers are the product of an explosion in population following World War II. Many developed countries around the world experienced their own baby booms. In Canada, the baby boom is generally accepted to have occurred between 1946 and 1964. Those born between these times are considered baby boomers.

The first baby boomers to turn sixty-five and approach the "normal" age of retirement did so in 2011. Since then, the population of seniors is only growing. In 2014, the over-sixty-five population was 14.8 percent of the total Canadian population. Compare that to what it was in 1971: 8 percent.

It's clear that Canada, as a country, is skewing older. In fact, forecasts indicate that in the next twenty years, almost one-third of all Canadians will be sixty-five and older. Right now, the median age in Canada is 40.6. In 1961, at the height of the baby boom, the median age was 26.3. That's a big difference.

What's clear is that a large portion of the population is entering retirement at once—and the trend is likely to continue over the course of the next sixteen years as more baby boomers reach age sixty-five. While Canadians aren't forced to retire when they reach age sixty-five, many of them are ready to do so, deciding to quit the daily grind and live a preferred lifestyle.

But are baby boomers ready for retirement? Careful planning is needed, not only because a large segment of the population is ready to retire, but because retirees are living longer than ever before. If you are approaching retirement right now, your money has to last considerably longer than your grandparents' money had to last.

The changing face of retirement

For those born two generations ahead of the current baby boomers, retirement was likely to last only five years. Back in 1920, the average life expectancy for males was fifty-nine, and for females it was sixty-one. They didn't even reach the retirement age we view as normal for today!

In 2014, the average life expectancy for Canadians had risen to seventy-nine for males and eighty-three for females. That means, if you retire at age sixty-five, you are likely to live another fourteen years if you are male and another eighteen years if you are female.

Canada- Life Expectancy at Birth			
Date	Life Expectancy	Life Expectancy- Men	Life Expectancy-Women
2014	81.47	79.38	83.74
2012	81.24	79.14	83.44
2010	80.89	78.73	83.16
2008	80.54	78.31	82.89
2006	80.64	78.40	83.00
2004	80.14	77.80	82.60
2002	79.59	77.20	82.10
2000	79.24	76.70	81.90
1998	78.66	75.96	81.50
1996	78.23	75.45	81.15
1994	77.86	74.94	80.93
1992	77.32	74.75	80.02
1990	77.38	74.26	80.65
1988	76.81	73.58	80.20
1986	76.44	73.24	79.80
1984	76.32	73.02	79.78
1982	75.68	72.30	79.23
1980	75.08	71.60	78.73
1978	74.53	70.92	78.32
1976	73.86	70.30	77.59
1974	73.24	69.74	76.91
1972	72.93	69.49	76.55
1970	72.70	69.32	76.25
1968	72.35	69.09	75.78
1966	72.00	68.78	75.39
1964	71.78	68.63	75.08
1962	71.37	68.45	74.43
1960	71.13	68.26	74.14

The reality, though, is that you are likely to live even beyond today's average life expectancy. With the advances in science, medicine, technology, and quality of life, it's very possible that you will live at least thirty years during your retirement. The thought of living until you are ninety-five is not so far-fetched these days. The face of retirement is changing into something with many more wrinkles than in the past.

If you are going to live until you are ninety-five—and perhaps beyond—you need to be prepared. You need a solid plan for your money. The worst thing that can happen is that you outlive your money and find yourself with a declining quality of life, exacerbated by your lack of funds. A good plan now is essential for a successful retirement later.

Every retirement is different

It's important, as you consider your future, to plan for *your* retirement. Each person has his or her own idea of what retirement should look like. The way you plan will determine whether or not you have sufficient funds to meet your individual goals in retirement.

Carefully think about what you want your retirement to look like, and don't forget to consider the following factors that can affect your overall retirement:

Lifestyle: Take the time to think about your preferred lifestyle. Some retirees like to travel the world. Others want to stay close to home and spend time with their children and grandchildren. Many retirees pick up new hobbies along the way or decide to learn a new skill. There are even those who decide to go back to college and earn a new degree! And, for some retirees, all of these elements are included in the desired retirement lifestyle.

All lifestyle choices are different, and they come with different costs. If you plan to stay at home most of the time, you might not need as large a nest egg as someone who wants to travel the world. If your hobby is fishing, you are likely to be able to enjoy it without incurring the same costs you would if you picked up golf as a hobby.

Your lifestyle preferences will dictate your retirement costs. The longer you enjoy your lifestyle, the more money you will need. Plan ahead so that you are able enjoy your retirement with the quality of life you have come to expect.

Health: One of the biggest concerns for retiring baby boomers is health. While the health system in Canada ensures that you will receive health care for your pressing medical needs, there might be times when you will want to pay out of your own pocket for health care. If you want a nonessential procedure performed faster, or if you want something specific done, you will need to pay for private care—and perhaps even head south of the border to the United States, where you will pay more for health care.

Another consideration for those who travel south for the winter is the fact that you need to purchase an extension of your health coverage if you are out of Canada for a longer period of time. If you don't make it back to Canada within the prescribed period of time, you will be required to purchase extended coverage. That's something to think about if you want to winter in Arizona or Florida.

Naturally, your health will also play a large role in whether or not you enjoy a certain quality of life. If you want the best possible quality of life, you need to take care of your health. This can mean certain costs that aren't covered in your health benefits as a Canadian citizen. You might want to join a gym or hire a personal trainer to help you stay on the right track. You might also want to buy certain vitamins or eat healthier (and costlier) foods.

Take a look at your health needs and consider how the costs might add up. You can't just assume that Canada's health system will completely cover all of your health needs.

Family issues: We all have different family issues that can affect our day-to-day lives. These issues don't just disappear in retirement. You might have adult children struggling financially. Perhaps you have a special-needs child who still needs care and help, even though you are aging. Your life partner might be in poor health, or you might even be experiencing a major life change of some sort.

Every family situation is different, and you need to consider how that might affect your retirement. Family issues can dictate what activities you feel you are able to participate in, as well as how much money you have at your disposal. Additionally, there are family issues that require you to engage in estate planning to ensure that your dependents are properly cared for even after you are gone.

Investments: Your investments can make a big difference in the way your retirement turns out. Your investment portfolio can provide you with enough money to live on practically indefinitely, or it can mean that you outlive your money. In order to ensure that you can live the lifestyle you want, keep up with your health, and address your family issues, you need to choose your investments carefully.

The right mix of investments combines a certain level of modest growth with a degree of safety. With a little help from a financial professional, it's possible to create a portfolio that protects some of your capital while growing your nest egg a little bit. Pay attention to your investments now, and make sure that you make a plan for how to continue investing in retirement. You'll need to shift your asset allocation as you approach retirement (and during retirement) so that you get the best possible results.

Tax considerations: Finally, your tax situation will have a big impact on how long your money lasts during retirement. Where you keep your money, as well as your income, can influence how much you pay in taxes. You want to put together a tax strategy designed to help you keep more of your money.

While you want to do your duty and pay your taxes, there is no reason to pay *more* than you have to. Meet with a financial professional who can help you with tax planning in retirement. There are certain tools and financial strategies you can use to manage your assets so that you reduce your tax liability. This is a vital part of your overall financial success in retirement.

Making the transition

One of the big choices you will need to make is whether or not you will jump right into full retirement. The factors listed above, from lifestyle to tax considerations, will influence whether or not you should jump right in or ease into retirement.

Are you in a position to retire completely?

You need to ask yourself whether or not you are really in a position to retire completely. Just reaching the age sixty-five doesn't automatically guarantee that you will be able to retire. Family issues might mean that you need to continue working beyond the age sixty-five. If your investments decrease just before you plan to retire, you might need to put off retirement until your portfolio recovers a bit.

If you have a spouse, you will also need to consider how retirement will affect him or her. If you retire before your spouse, there are challenges that you will need to overcome. Think about the possibility of retiring together so that you don't run into the disconnect that can come when one of you is retired while the other continues to work. It might make sense for you to continue working—at least part-time—for a couple more years if it means that you and your spouse can enjoy your time together.

IS IT TIME YET?

Before you retire, take a look at your financial situation and consider that you might need to extend your working years, or work part-time. A good financial professional can give you some good ideas about asset management and help you explore your options.

Are you emotionally ready to retire completely?

Many retirees actually find it difficult to transition to retirement. It's not as easy as you might think to quit your job and then wake up the next morning with nothing to do. Most of us might dream about having nothing to do all day, but after a few days of living that dream, it becomes monotonous.

One of the biggest problems with full retirement is the isolation and loneliness. Studies show that older adults benefit from social interaction. These benefits are mental and emotional and can even affect physical health. If you are used to social interaction at work, and then you suddenly end up without those connections, it can be problematic. You can keep working (at least part-time) to maintain those social ties, or you can find other activities to engage in. Many seniors find it beneficial to get involved with different community groups or make friends so that they fill that need for social interaction.

Emotionally, you might not actually be ready to stop work altogether. Switching to full retirement can require a serious transition. Many retirees find that they don't have the same sense of purpose after retiring. A job offers a sense that you are doing something to benefit society—and that you are needed and appreciated.

It can make sense to work part-time and transition slowly. Start by cutting your hours a bit so that you are working a little less. Then, drop to part-time work. Finally, you can retire fully, depending on your readiness.

However, your only options aren't to retire fully or to work part-time. It's also possible to find other ways to find fulfillment in your life. You can do volunteer work as a way to provide vital services to others. One of the great things about volunteering is that you don't need to worry about earning money; you can just concentrate on using your skills and talents to help others.

Some retirees find "fun" jobs as local history interpreters, tour guides, consultants, or seasonal workers. It's possible to find this kind of work and enjoy it without worrying too much about whether or not you receive a great deal of compensation.

In the end, many seniors continue some sort employment not because they need the money, but because they enjoy interacting with other people and because they want to feel useful. Make sure you take this into account as you prepare to retire. Your retirement might look different from your parents' and grandparents' retirement due to the longer lifespan and your better health and quality of life. There's no reason to think that you have to follow a "traditional" retirement path.

Can you retire with debt?

In the past, retiring with debt was seen as a big negative. However, more and more Canadians are retiring with some debt. One of the most common debts that Canadians retire with is a mortgage.

With the expanding mortgage products and options available, many Canadians are starting to pay on their homes longer. And, with the ultra-low mortgage rates right now, it's affordable for many retirees to quit their jobs, or at least cut back their hours dramatically, and still manage their mortgage payments without too much trouble.

Even though mortgage rates are at fifty-year lows, this state of affairs won't last forever. Eventually mortgage rates will rise. And what happens if the housing market turns out to be in a bubble? Many think that the housing market is still heating up too fast and that a crash may be coming. For some Canadians—including those who are retired or close to retirement—that could be a real problem. You need a plan to account for the possibility of rising mortgage rates (and the higher payments that come with higher mortgage rates).

On top of that, if you have other debt, you need to be prepared for that as well. The consumer debt load continues to grow at a rapid pace in Canada, and that includes credit card debt. Recent information indicates that the debt load in Canada is growing 400 percent faster than inflation. As a result, more and more Canadians are nearing retirement with debt.

As long as you can handle the payments, and as long as interest rates are relatively low, this isn't much of an issue for most retirees. However, the situation gets dicey if rates rise, or if you see too much of your nest egg being diverted to keep up with debt payments. You need a plan to pay down your debt if you can and protect yourself against interest rate increases that are surely coming in the future.

Why planning is key

In order to ensure that you can meet the challenges that come with modern retirement, you need a good plan. The right financial strategy can ensure that you don't outlive your money—but do so in comfort. Here are some of the aspects of the right approach to the new Canadian retirement:

Retirement projections: There are plenty of retirement projectors out there. These tools are designed to help you calculate likely retirement scenarios. You can determine how much money you need to set aside each month in order to meet your retirement goals. It's also possible to project how much your portfolio is likely to grow from now until you retire.

There are many sophisticated tools out there that can help you account for taxes and inflation as well as possible returns. Too many people neglect to consider taxes and inflation when planning for retirement. However, it's vital that you consider these factors. If you are unsure about using online forecasters, consider getting the help of a knowledge-able financial planner. The right adviser can help you see exactly where you stand now and figure out where you are headed in the future.

It's important that you keep your estimates on the conservative side in order to achieve more realistic results. Don't assume that the stock por-tion of your RRSP is going to return 10 percent annually. The reality is that you are far more likely to see relatively conservative returns of 6 to 7 percent. Planning based on these more conservative numbers will give you a better chance of success.

Likewise, you have a better chance of success with your retirement plan-ning when you make conservative estimates with taxes and inflation. Assume you will have to pay higher taxes and consider that slightly higher inflation will erode your purchasing power. It's better to overplan and be pleasantly surprised later, than to take a too-rosy view now and outlive your money during retirement.

Tax-friendly retirement: While you should save your money as if taxes are going to take a big bite out of your retirement, you shouldn't just accept the idea of paying them. Even though you will want to assume the worst when you make retirement projections, you shouldn't resign yourself to the worst.

Instead, look for ways to adopt tax-friendly strategies that can reduce your tax bill in retirement. The right tax planning can mean that you keep a lot more of your money. Improper tax planning can cost you thousands of dollars in lost retirement income. It's worth it to consult a knowledgeable professional about structuring your assets so that you minimize the amount of tax you pay.

You don't want to do anything illegal, though. This is where the right tax planning or financial planning professional can help. He or she can ensure that you take advantage of perfectly legal ways to lower your tax bill and keep more of your hard-earned cash for your benefit during the golden years of retirement.

Do you have enough?: Before you retire, make sure that you have enough. Consider your sources of income. Do you have a part-time job you can rely on? Did you start a business, and is there income from that? What about dividend stocks? Is your portfolio large enough to generate reliable income? Can you expect an inheritance?

All of these are questions you should ask yourself. Generally, it's not wise to rely on things like inheritances and other windfalls to fund your retirement. However, you will want to consider the impact that such windfalls can have on your tax situation and your overall retirement picture. Before you do anything with an inheritance or other windfall, step back and consider your options. Get some good advice from someone who understands how finances work and can help you navigate your options.

Also consider other factors that can affect whether or not you have enough to retire. Look at where your money is coming from and what expenses you will have. The goal should be to plan ahead and construct a retirement portfolio that can stand the test of time.

Baby boomers—and following generations—are likely to live decades longer than many of the generations before. This longer life expectancy means that your retirement will last a good portion of your life. It's not unreasonable to think that you could spend a quarter of your life or more in retirement. This means that planning is essential. You need to get on track now, before retirement, and you need to have a good plan in place to help you get through retirement in comfort.

You need to make sure that you don't outlive your money.

CHAPTER TWO:

GENERATING RETIREMENT INCOME

You need a plan

If you expect to experience a successful retirement, you need a plan. The good news is that it doesn't need to be difficult or complicated. I have been using the same retirement income planning process for more than twenty-five years. While many of the variables have changed over the years, including interest rates, taxes, and returns, the process in arriving at a successful retirement income plan remains the same.

In fact, the process for creating a good retirement income plan is the same no matter what stage a retiree is at. Following the process provides tangible efficiencies, allowing you to enjoy tax savings, income consistency, and peace of mind.

Building your retirement income plan can be accomplished in five steps:

1. Evaluate your current net worth.
2. Assess your current retirement and lifestyle objectives.
3. Establish financial goals.
4. Create the retirement income that will allow you to reach your goals.
5. Coordinate your income plan with your current assets.

Once you have followed this process, you will have an income plan that allows you to live comfortably and establish the lifestyle of your choosing.

How do I get started?

Your first step is to decide that you are ready to begin making a plan. This is something you can do right now. The process starts when you— the retiree—are ready to plan for income during retirement. Make the decision to put together a plan for your retirement.

Detailed input is required during what I like to call the "discovery process." This process is all about you. Not only do you need to take a look at your financial data, but you also need to consider more nuanced items. Softer data, including time horizons, past experiences, risk tolerance, and current knowledge, are also considered during this time.

Not only does the discovery process include digging into your current situation, but it also involves your hopes for the future and your goals. What lifestyle do you hope to be living in the next five years? This is the kind of information that we need to have before making a plan. Part of the discovery process is figuring out exactly where you are now and where you hope to be. That way, it's possible to create a plan that bridges the gap.

Gathering all of the data you need during the discovery process is a significant task that requires time and effort. You need to gather all financial statements that you have, as well as information on any assets that you possess. You also need to take the time to really think about your financial life, and what you want it to look like.

The more accurate and complete your data is, and the clearer you are about your objectives, the more complete your retirement income plan will be.

Step 1: Evaluate your current net worth

The first step in creating your successful retirement income plan is understanding your present situation. One of the best ways to get an idea of where you stand right now is to evaluate your current net worth.

Your current net worth represents a snapshot of your finances right now. This can be useful if you want to have a good idea of your starting point. Normally, when figuring net worth, you subtract your liabilities from your assets. However, when making a plan for retirement income, I suggest taking a look at your assets in terms of what will actually produce income on your behalf. It's a modified approach to evaluating your net worth.

From a retirement income planning standpoint, I don't consider your home, cottage, or car as assets. They don't produce income that you can use to live off during retirement. The ideal situation is to identify assets that have the potential to continue to grow during retirement so you can support your lifestyle.

You can even consider slowly diminishing investments assets as part of your positive net worth. However, it's important to consider these slowly diminishing assets as part of a plan. Why were these assets accumulated in the first place? Did you expect them to diminish over time? In many cases, slowly diminishing assets can be a part of your estate planning efforts.

Take a look at all of your assets. Which can be expected to provide you with income? How long can you expect to receive income as a result of these assets? When looking at your current net worth, you need to evaluate your income-producing assets as well as recognize some of the liabilities that you have.

In general, the goal at this stage is to figure out which assets to shore up so that they continue producing income and which liabilities can be eliminated and replaced by income-producing assets. Evaluating your net worth can help you get a feel for where you stand and help you identify your financial holdings in terms of income-producing assets and in terms of liabilities.

As part of this consideration, you will also need to look at your life expectancy. While most Canadians know that they will likely live until they are in their eighties, it's important to plan out for even longer than that. Health advances continue to increase longevity, so the fact that your life expectancy might only be seventy-nine right now doesn't account for the fact that in ten more years, your life expectancy is likely to bump up a little higher.

Too many Canadians outlive their money because they live longer than expected. Don't let that happen to you. It makes sense to plan out to at least age ninety. It's much better to have your money outlive you than it is to outlive your money and find your quality of life rapidly deteriorating.

After you consider your life expectancy and whether or not your current assets can get you to ninety (or beyond), you need to think about what you hope to leave behind for your posterity. Part of evaluating your net worth, and the types of assets you have, is looking at the tax situation. Are your assets tax efficient? When your estate passes on, will it do so with minimal hassle and without the government taking more than it's strictly entitled to?

To evaluate your assets, look at your liabilities. Figure out which assets are inefficient in terms of tax and estate planning, and then prepare to make adjustments so that your assets are protected for the long term.

Step 2: Assess your current retirement and lifestyle objectives

Now that you know where you stand with your finances and with your assets, it's time to determine what you want to accomplish with these resources. Look at your current retirement objectives and consider what you want to do with your life.

Retirement, in many ways, is about lifestyle design. A successful retirement isn't just about surviving day to day; it's about living the life that makes you happiest. As a result, you need to consider the following factors as you create retirement and lifestyle objectives—and remember that it's not just about the money.

Will you work?

Many retirees find that they aren't quite ready to withdraw entirely from the social connections that come with work. The issue of whether or not you will work for some part of your retirement is a major concern. Your employment status represents income, and it also affects tax issues.

A number of seniors find retirement an ideal time to try something new as well. It is common to work part-time in an enjoyable, but low-paying, job during retirement. You have the chance to interact with coworkers as well as earn a little extra money and improve your cash flow. You can also continue to build assets when you work during retirement.

Think about what work you might enjoy if money were no object, and then consider doing that during retirement.

Where will you live?

Your living situation can play a large role in the rate at which you go through your nest egg during retirement. If you live in an expensive city, you will need more assets to sustain your lifestyle. There are many cost-efficient localities in Canada that can help you stretch your retirement dollar.

Other living situations to consider include:

- Downsizing: Many retirees decide to sell larger homes and use the proceeds to buy smaller homes. You might not need a bigger house.
- Second home: Do you want to be able to have a second home? You will need more assets if you want to maintain two homes.
- Travel: This is a popular mode of living for many retirees. If you plan to travel, you need to consider whether you want a "home base" or not. You can also decide to get an RV and travel around—but you'll have costs associated with that as well.
- International living: Consider, too, whether or not you want to spend time in other countries. Many Canadians head to the southern United States during the winter months, and others enjoy world travel and living. However, you will need to consider additional costs and understand the consequences on your access to health care if you spend long periods of time outside Canada.

- Retirement communities: Also consider the feasibility of retirement and assisted-living communities. Understand the costs associated with these types of living arrangements.

Where you live has a big impact—it influences what activities you have access to, as well as dictates what you will pay for food, transportation, and housing. Think about your preferred lifestyle and what type of living arrangement would best reflect your priorities and objectives.

How will you spend your time?

One of the biggest challenges faced by retirees is figuring out what to *do* with all the time that's been freed up now that the day job is done. Even if you work for a portion of your retirement, at some point you'll start reducing your hours on the job and start spending time elsewhere.

It helps to have a plan for your time. While it might be relaxing to do nothing but watch TV for a week or two, that can become tedious and boring after a while. Instead, think about what activities can give your retirement meaning.

Do you have a hobby? Would you like to go back to school and learn something new or get another degree? Do you want to volunteer and make a difference in your community? Would you like to travel the world and meet new people? These are all activities that can give meaning to your daily schedule and enhance your quality of life, and you can choose any—or all—of them to be part of your retirement.

Think about what your ideal day would be like and consider how you can make that happen. Recognize, too, that some activities are more expensive than others and that it can make sense to plan your finances accordingly. You will need to make sure that you have the income during retirement to support the ability to spend your time as you like.

How will your spouse deal with your retirement?

While it's common to think about how you will spend *your* time and think about what *you* can accomplish now that you have the means to do what you want, many retirees neglect to think about how retirement will affect a life partner.

First of all, when you retire at different times, it can make things difficult in your household. Your partner has to adjust to the reduction in income now that you no longer have your day job. Additionally, what happens if you want to do one thing, but your partner is restricted by a job? Finally, it's important to think about how your interactions as a couple might change. Many couples find that they have a hard time adjusting to spending so much time together. Now that the kids are gone and no longer providing a distraction, and now that jobs are no longer taking them out of the house, the time spent together can be truly eye-opening.

Before you get too far into the retirement planning process, it's important to speak with your partner. Do you both have the same lifestyle objectives for this stage of your life? You and your partner need to be on the same page and have the same goals if you want a successful and satisfying retirement.

Health issues

Don't forget to consider health issues. While Canada's health care system is generally adequate for most situations, there are times when you might need to pursue private options—either in Canada, or south of the border in the United States. Think, too, about the impact of your health on your quality of life. Poor health can mean greater expenses, and it can also mean that you are unable to enjoy some of the activities you hoped to participate in during retirement.

Make sure that you factor the possibility of poor health into your retirement planning calculations. You should also plan to do what you can to maintain good health for as long as possible. It will be less costly in the long run, and you'll enjoy yourself much more if you have good health.

Take steps before retirement to improve your health by including appropriate exercise and nutrition. A long retirement is practically a prison sentence if you don't have the ability to enjoy a good quality of life.

Step 3: Establish financial goals

You have evaluated your current situation, and now you know what type of lifestyle you want during retirement. Your next step is to establish financial goals that will ensure that you are able to enjoy the retirement lifestyle you envision for yourself.

As you consider financial benchmarks for your retirement, you need to consider the following issues:

- Inflation: As prices increase over time, your purchasing power is eroded. The future value of your dollar is less than its present value. You need to set financial goals that help you overcome the effects of inflation and retain your purchasing power throughout retirement. The good news is that the **CPP** and **OAS**, as well as some private pensions, are indexed to inflation. The right approach in this manner can help you preserve your purchasing power.
- Longevity: How long will you live? Your main financial goal in retirement is to create a situation in which you don't outlive your

money. Remember that life expectancies are increasing, so you might live longer than you expect.

- Taxes: Another important financial goal is improving your tax efficiency. Reduce your taxes and you will keep more of your money, allowing you to enjoy a better quality of life and decrease the chances of outliving your funds. While you don't want to illegally avoid taxes, you do want to make it a point to legally reduce your tax liability.
- Wealth transfer: Many retirees have goals to leave something behind. This means that a wealth transfer plan needs to be in place.
- Health-risk management: Finally, don't forget that your financial objectives also need to include a way to manage the monetary risk that comes with health issues. As you age, you will run into health problems; there is no avoiding this. Your financial objectives need to address this issue.

When you keep the above factors in mind, you can set more realistic financial goals that you have a better chance of achieving.

Planning for the survivor

While it's never pleasant to think of the death of a loved one, it's important that you consider what your financial situation will look like if your partner passes on before you do. You need to consider what income will be lost if your partner dies and whether or not you will have the cash flow needed to meet your needs.

Think about the impact the lack of your partner will have on your current benefits. You should also consider this possibility for your partner. If you are the one to die, you want your partner to be able to continue living in comfort during retirement.

Consider the possible changes to an investment plan if one of you dies. Also, realize that being a survivor means that you need to make changes

to beneficiary information. Most retirees name their partner as beneficiary for many accounts. However, once your partner is gone, you will
need to designate a new beneficiary.

Cash flow in retirement

How will your money move through your personal economy during retirement? Think about the expenses you are likely to encounter during
retirement and consider those in relation to the income that you can
expect.

Some costs, such as the need to buy clothes for work, as well as transportation costs related to commuting, disappear with retirement.
Additionally, if you have worked to pay down debt, you will have few
obligations during retirement.

These reduced expenses, though, are often balanced by a change in situation. You no longer have active income (or you have reduced active
income); instead, you are drawing on your assets. Over time, your accounts can become depleted. You will need to balance the situation so
that you have adequate income for your needs.

As part of your cash flow analysis in retirement, don't forget to consider taxes. Any employment income you have during this time is
fully taxable. You can reduce your tax liability by carefully considering other types of income. While income from interest, pensions,
and **RRIFs** are fully taxable, there are ways to improve your tax
efficiency with the help of return of capital, dividends, and capital
gains.

Estimate the costs involved to meet your retirement and lifestyle objectives, and then consider how you will cover those costs.

Step 4: Create the retirement income that will allow you to reach your goals

After you have figured out what your cash flow will probably look like in retirement, it's time to determine how you will get the income you need to make it happen.

Put your assets to work

Remember, in Step 1 you evaluated your different assets and income sources. Now is the time to make a plan to put those assets to work for you. Try to look for ways to keep your benefits and assets producing income on your behalf. If you can generate high-enough returns, you won't have to rely as much on your capital. The less you rely on your capital to fund your retirement, the longer your money will last.

Look for income-producing investments that can help you generate decent income. Consider sources that offer a mix of potentially higher returns, as well as safe-income generators like GICs. You can create a portfolio of income assets that offers continued growth during retirement, while being balanced out to some degree by assets that are considered a little safer.

Be tax smart

It's essential that you consider the tax implications of your income plan. Remember that the income from the following items is fully taxable:

- CPP
- OAS
- LIF
- LRIF
- RLIF

- RRIF
- Pensions
- Interest from non-registered assets

A good strategy is to draw on these assets first. That way, you can increase your chances that they will be taxed at a lower tax rate. Order matters when you begin withdrawing from your various accounts and receiving benefits.

Be aware of your tax bracket in retirement. A higher tax bracket can mean that you have to make adjustments in your expectations for the type of retirement lifestyle you lead.

Employ strategies to legally reduce your tax liability. Many couples find that using income-splitting and asset-splitting strategies can help reduce overall household tax liability. In some cases, it's possible to split your income and assets in such a way that your partner takes on some of your tax liability. If your partner is in a lower tax bracket, you can reduce the overall tax liability of your household with strategic splitting. Find out from a qualified professional how this can help you make the most of your income during retirement.

Step 5: Coordinate your income plan with your current assets

As soon as you create a future income plan, it's time to coordinate that plan with the reality of where you are starting out right now.

It's important to understand that capital preservation is of the utmost importance. As a baby boomer, your time to earn is running out. Capital preservation is about making sure that your initial money stays safe. You are past the point where you have time to recover from stock market drops.

While you do want to include a component of return in your portfolio, hopefully helping you generate a little more income for later, it's secondary to capital preservation. At the very least, you need to ensure that your initial investment is mostly safe.

Asset allocation

One of the most important factors in determining your success in retirement is asset allocation. Asset allocation is an important part of any investing plan, no matter your time of life. As your retirement progresses, your asset allocation should shift.

During retirement, your asset allocation should focus on the following three asset classes:

1. Cash: This is considered the safest of all asset classes. Cash is very liquid. You can access it quickly and easily. However, just because cash is considered "safe" doesn't mean there aren't downsides. The biggest disadvantage is that cash offers a very low yield. In some cases, the yield is so low that it doesn't keep up with the rate of inflation. You may not lose your nominal capital, but the way that inflation erodes your purchasing can lead to a loss in real terms. Keep a portion of your portfolio in cash, though, for accessibility and safety purposes.

2. Fixed-income: These are assets that provide you with a set rate of return. Fixed-income assets like GICs, bonds, and certain fixed-income funds provide you with predictable returns. These returns usually beat what you would see with cash, but they are still far from the types of returns that result in dramatic growth. The bulk of your retirement portfolio should be in fixed-income assets that can provide you with the guarantee of capital preservation on top of regular cash flow.

3. Equities: Stocks can provide you with a growth component in your retirement portfolio. It is this part of your portfolio that can

GENERATING RETIREMENT INCOME

help you beat inflation and help your nest egg see a measure of growth even though you are retired. The downside to equities is that they are more volatile than cash and are fixed-income assets. With the potential for bigger gains and growth comes the equal potential for bigger losses. You don't want to lean too heavily on equities for a retirement portfolio, since a couple of bad years in the stock market can wipe out a good portion of your nest egg.

Understand that timing matters, too. You want to lower the overall volatility of your portfolio just prior to your retirement and in the early years of your portfolio. Studies show that a major market event during the first few years of your portfolio can have a bigger negative impact on your portfolio than if that market event happened later on.

Age	Year	Scenario #1		Scenario #2		Scenario #3	
		Rate of Return	*Negative Returns First	Rate of Return	*Flat Rate of Return	Rate of Return	*Positive Returns First
65	1	-7.0%	$430,000	6.0%	$494,991	16.1%	$545,700
66	2	-7.0%	$363,850	6.0%	$488,632	16.1%	$597,508
67	3	-7.0%	$301,249	6.0%	$480,809	16.1%	$656,575
68	4	9.2%	$290,718	6.0%	$471,404	9.2%	$678,734
69	5	9.2%	$278,072	6.0%	$460,287	9.2%	$701,785
70	6	9.2%	$263,080	6.0%	$447,321	9.2%	$725,775
71	7	9.2%	$245,491	6.0%	$432,361	9.2%	$750,754
72	8	16.1%	$241,970	6.0%	$415,249	-7.0%	$655,156
73	9	16.1%	$236,590	6.0%	$395,820	-7.0%	$564,958
74	10	16.1%	$229,109	6.0%	$373,895	-7.0%	$479,744
Avg. Annualized Return		6.00%		6.00%		6.00%	
Value at end of 10 years			$229,109		$373,895		$479,744

*Based on $500,000 beginning portfolio balance

Source: Standard & Poor's. This example is hypothetical and is for illustrative purposes only. It assumes a 6.0% average annualized rate of return, rounded to the first decimal, and 7% annual withdrawal based on the first-year principal, adjusted thereafter for 3% inflation each year. Actual results will vary. Past performance does not guarantee future results.

Lower volatility is vital as you move into retirement, since losses early in retirement can cause problems with the long-term viability of your portfolio.

Taxes and fees

Don't forget to consider taxes and fees as you coordinate your current and future plans for your money. You should work to reduce the fees you pay, since they directly reduce your returns. Look for ways to streamline your portfolio and check for low-cost investments. In many cases, it's possible for you to employ low-cost alternatives to assets that currently charge higher fees.

Your asset allocation should also consider the expected tax situation. Whenever possible, interest-bearing assets should be held in registered plans in order to reap the tax benefits. Dividend and capital gains investments come with tax advantages, so keeping them in registered plans is counterproductive. Instead, these investment vehicles should be kept in nonregistered plans as much as possible.

Work with an expert planner to help you figure out how to best avoid fees and reduce your taxes over time.

Transferring wealth

Also, consider how you can transfer your wealth to survivors efficiently and painlessly. Your coordination should include your partner's assets as well as your own. Retirement income planning should include a comprehensive action plan so that the surviving partner in a couple can maintain the desired lifestyle.

Get help planning your wealth transfer to your heirs as well. Complete estate planning should be part of the process. Now is the time to set up your estate plan, ensuring that your assets are used the way you want them used after you pass on.

Don't forget to get help creating a plan for protecting your financial interests if you become incapacitated as well. These items might seem a little boring, but they are of the utmost importance—especially if you want to maintain your legacy.

Withdrawing your retirement income

Your coordination plan is incomplete without an understanding of how much you should withdraw. Your rate of withdrawal from your retirement investment accounts should be sustainable over a long period of time.

The general rule of thumb is that if you can keep your withdrawals to 4 percent of your assets each year, your money is more likely to last indefinitely when you consider an average return of 7 percent on all your assets and subtract 3 percent to account for inflation.

If you withdraw less than 4 percent of your assets each year, your retirement is often considered "overfunded." While it seems strange to think that you can have "too much" for retirement, the fact that you can live the life you want without withdrawing more than 4 percent of your assets each year means that you have excess.

A withdrawal rate of between 4 percent and 7 percent a year indicates "constrained" funds. You need to make sure that you watch your expenditures so that you don't end up outliving your money.

If your lifestyle requires that you withdraw more than 7 percent of your assets each year, your retirement is considered "underfunded." You probably don't have enough money to last your lifetime, since you are more than likely drawing on your capital for a significant portion of your income.

It's important to understand that rules of thumb offer good guidance, but every case is different. If you don't mind drawing down your assets at a more rapid rate, and you aren't concerned with leaving anything for survivors, you might not care if you are tapping into your original capital and withdrawing money at a rate of more than 7 percent of your assets each year. Every case is different.

On top of that, there are factors that can further complicate withdrawal rates:

- Changing taxation, including the possibility that the government will raise taxes while you are retired.
- Financial crises that result in portfolio losses and difficult economic conditions.
- Changes to your own life objectives.
- Changes to your marital status, resulting in the loss of assets and legal costs.
- Commitment to helping adult children. Many retirees find themselves unexpectedly dealing with the challenges of helping adult children.
- Health changes, which can adjust your living situation as well as incur costs.
- Death of your spouse, resulting in changes to your asset base and other costs that might be incurred.

Your withdrawal rate needs to be evaluated regularly, along with your asset allocation. As conditions change, you might need to make adjustments to the makeup of your retirement portfolio, as well as change your rate of withdrawal.

GENERATING RETIREMENT INCOME

Meet with your financial advisor regularly to ensure that you are still on track with your finances. Make periodic changes to your portfolio so that you remain on top of the situation.

CHAPTER THREE:

THE THREE SOURCES OF RETIREMENT INCOME

Where does your retirement income come from?

Once you quit your job, you will need a way to replace your income. There are three main sources of retirement income:

1. Government
2. Employer
3. Personal

THE THREE SOURCES OF RETIREMENT INCOME

Your retirement strategy should consider each source of income and how large a role it will play in ensuring that you are financially stable throughout your golden years.

Government income

The Canadian government has put into place policies designed to help you during retirement. While this is helpful in terms of making sure that most Canadians don't end up living in terrible conditions, the government portion of your retirement income isn't meant to completely replace the income from your day job.

While a government check can supplement your income, it doesn't make sense to rely entirely on what the government offers, since the amount you receive might be reduced according to your income level. Plan ahead to rely on some of your individual savings and investments as well as what you receive from the government.

The two main sources of retirement income from the government are Old Age Security and the Canada Pension Plan.

Old Age Security (OAS)

OAS is the main program associated with Canada's retirement support system. If you have been living in Canada for at least ten years after turning eighteen, you are eligible for a modest payment at the age of sixty-five—or sixty if you can show that you are low-income and need the money.

OAS - Changes to the age of eligibility. Starting in April 2023, the age of eligibility for the Old Age Security and Guaranteed Income Supplement (GIS) will gradually increase from 65 to 67 over six years, with full implementation by January 2029. This change will affect people born in 1958 and later.

You are required to apply if you want your benefits, though. Even if you are still working, or even if you have never worked, you can apply for OAS benefits. Eligibility depends on your legal status, how old you are, and how many years you have lived in Canada.

Even if you don't live in Canada right now, you might still be eligible for OAS. If you were a Canadian citizen or legal resident the day before you left the country, and if you have lived in Canada for at least twenty years after turning eighteen, it's possible to receive your benefits.

Realize that you might not receive OAS benefits if you are incarcerated. If you are incarcerated due to a sentence of at least two years in a federal penitentiary, or a sentence of at least ninety days in provincial or territorial facilities, you can't receive benefits during incarceration.

As of July 1, 2013, it's possible to delay the receipt of your benefits for up to five years. This can increase your pension amount by 0.6 percent for each month that you delay your pension, capping at 36 percent total at age seventy. It's also possible to receive delayed benefits retroactively after July 1, 2013.

Realize, too, that the amount of your OAS payment can be reduced depending on your income. The income amount changes, usually in line with inflation. For every dollar above the income level, the amount of your OAS pension is reduced by $0.15. If you have received your payments already during the year, you need to repay the so-called clawback amount.

THE THREE SOURCES OF RETIREMENT INCOME

Canada Pension Plan (CPP)

In addition to OAS, there is the CPP. Employed Canadians eighteen years and older have a portion of their income automatically contributed to the social insurance program known as the CPP. Those who are self-employed also pay into the CPP based on their net business income.

The CPP is operated on behalf of all of the provinces and territories in Canada, except Quebec, which has its own plan. The CPP offers disability benefits, a retirement pension, and survivor benefits.

The minimum amount considered "pensionable" earnings is $3,500 and the maximum (year's maximum pension earnings, or YMPE) is adjusted each year, depending on the average wage. If you end up overpaying, you'll receive a refund at tax time.

Your contributions to the plan add up to "credits" each year. As a rule, the longer you contribute and the more that is contributed (as your income increases), the higher your benefit. If you are concerned about how low-earning years can reduce your benefit, there are ways to "drop out" some of the years from the calculation. The following spans of time can be excluded:

- Months of low earnings after the age of sixty-five
- 15 percent of the lowest-earning years in your contributory period
- Periods of time when you reduced your hours (and earnings) or stopped working as a result of your efforts to raise a child under the age of seven
- Months when you had eligibility for CPP disability benefits

Check your record of earnings regularly so that you know how much you have contributed and you can see where you stand in terms of benefits.

If your marriage or common-law partnership ends, something needs to be done about the pension credits earned during the marriage. The credits earned during the partnership can be split evenly between former partners in the event of separation or divorce—even if one of the partners hasn't contributed to the CPP.

You can also engage in pension sharing between spouses/common-law partners. With pension sharing, one partner can assign a portion of his or her pension to the other. This doesn't change the benefit, but it can have tax implications. Since CPP benefits are considered taxable income, some couples find that it makes sense to assign some of the CPP benefits of a higher-income partner to a lower-income spouse. That way, the total tax paid by the couple can be decreased.

If you die, a death benefit is paid out. It is calculated based on the amount that the CPP would have been if you had been age sixty-five at death. The benefit is worth six months' of benefits, with a cap at $2,500.

The survivor benefit is also something to take into consideration. A surviving spouse or common-law partner can receive survivor benefits based on disability status, what the contributor has paid into the plan (and for how long), and the age of the survivor at the time of the contributor's death. It's worth noting that remarriage doesn't end the survivor benefits.

Children can also receive survivor benefits if the deceased parent has paid into the system, meeting contributory requirements. The children's benefit is a flat monthly rate, adjusted each year according to inflation/ cost of living. It's possible for a child to receive two benefits in the event that both parents have paid into the CPP, and if each parent is deceased or disabled. A child under eighteen doesn't usually receive the benefit directly (although this is possible); usually, the guardian of the child receives the payment. A child over eighteen who meets full-time student status requirements can receive a direct payment.

When should I begin taking CPP benefits?

One of the questions you need to ask yourself is when it makes sense to take CPP benefits. It's possible to begin taking early pension benefits, but you want to make sure that it will work in your circumstance. For many retirees, though, taking your benefits earlier rather than later can be a smart move.

The "full" retirement age for beginning to take CPP benefits is sixty-five. However, you can start taking benefits at age sixty. If you do this, though, you will see a reduction of 31.2 percent of your benefits. However, if you put off receiving your benefits until you are seventy, you end up with a 30 percent increase in your monthly benefit.

Deciding how to proceed can present a bit of difficulty. How well it works out often depends on how long you expect to live. If you think that you will die relatively soon, it makes sense to begin taking CPP benefits as early as possible—starting at age sixty. However, if you think you might live longer, it can be tempting to put off taking your benefits until you are seventy.

However, even if you think that you are going to live to a good old age, it might make sense to begin taking your CPP benefits early. There are two main reasons to consider taking your CPP benefits early:

1. **Investment**: So what if you end up with 30 percent less in benefits by taking your benefits starting at age sixty? The reality is that you can take that money and invest it. Consider: you start

taking your pension checks at age sixty, so you receive sixty extra checks (even if they are for less). If your monthly pension payment is $400, that's $24,000 that you'll receive over that five years. Instead of spending it, consider investing it. With the right approach, you can use that $24,000 over the course of five years to harvest returns that exceed what you would have gotten if you waited until you were seventy.

2. **Income penalties later**: Another reality that you might have to face if you wait until you are seventy to begin taking CPP benefits is the penalties that can come with a higher income. That extra addition to your monthly benefit payment could mean higher taxes. And it might mean an OAS clawback to boot. If you think that higher income—especially if it's more than you need or will use—can pose problems later on, it makes sense to just start taking your CPP benefits as soon as possible.

Only you can decide what is likely to work best for you. If you wait until you are seventy to begin taking CPP benefits and you die at age seventy-two, you will have missed out on quite a bit of what you are entitled to. If you are more interested in making sure you get the most for your CPP contribution, starting early at sixty, or at least starting at the "full" retirement age of sixty-five, can make good sense in the long run.

CPP rule changes

It's also important to take into account the rule changes coming for CPPs, which started in 2013 and are being phased in through 2016. This can change the calculation for you just marginally.

The new change will decrease your benefits when you take them early, moving up to a 31.2 percent reduction in 2013 and gradually increasing to a reduction of 36 percent in 2016. The changes also affect the situation for those who wait until they are seventy to take their benefits. Eventually, the benefit for waiting will increase to 42 percent.

For some retirees, this might change the calculation a little bit. The government is trying to encourage you to put off taking your benefits for a little longer. Even with these rule changes, though, a savvy investor can still benefit from the power of compound returns by taking CPP benefits early and then investing the money.

It's possible to continue to contribute to the CPP even after you have reached the age of sixty-five. Those who work between the ages of sixty-five and seventy, and are receiving pension benefits, can still contribute. This contribution goes into the Post-Retirement Benefit (PRB). (Realize that you will be required to make PRB contributions if you work and receive benefits if you are between the ages of sixty and sixty-five. After the age of sixty-five, your contributions to PRB are optional.)

For some workers, it can make sense to begin taking CPP benefits early, even while working. You can take your benefits and continue to build toward your total retirement savings with the help of the PRB.

Carefully consider your situation, and decide what will work best for you in the long run. Your calculations should include not only what you get from the government, but also what you can expect to receive from company and individual retirement income sources.

Company income

Not only can you expect to receive money from the government, but you also might receive income as a result of your employment. Income from an employer can help support you during your retirement.

Often, company retirement income comes in the form of earned income (an actual job), pension income, and LIF income. You might also be eligible to receive severance income from your job, as well as other types of income.

Earned income

It's possible for you to keep working in retirement. For some retirees, this is actually a desirable development. If you are concerned about your income situation, a job can help ease your cash-flow problems while putting off the time that you need to rely entirely on your investment portfolio or the government.

Even having a part-time job can be helpful. If you start taking your CPP benefits early, and then have a part-time job, it might be able to help you get through until you are ready to begin withdrawing money from your RRSP.

Not only can earned income help you when it comes to your financial situation, but a job during retirement can be good for your mental and emotional well-being. Too many retirees find themselves at loose ends during retirement. Quality of life and length of life can be cut down when you don't feel like you have a purpose. Plus, the social interactions that you receive on the job can be good for your mental and emotional health during retirement.

Also, just because you have a job and just because you are receiving CPP benefits is no reason to stop contributing to your future. Earned income during retirement (even if it's just from a part-time job) can provide you a way to keep growing your nest egg through contributions to PRB.

Pension income

Some companies provide pension plans for Canadians. With an employer pension plan, the employer makes a contribution to a pension on your behalf. In some cases, you are required to make a matching contribution as well, depending on the plan.

The types of plans offered by employers fall into one of two categories:

1. **Defined Benefit Pension (DBP)**: With this type of plan, you receive a set benefit from your employer. Upon retirement this benefit is figured using your earnings at the time you retire as well as how long you have worked for the company. You, as the employee, have no active involvement in managing the plan. In some cases (particularly with public sector plans), payouts are also indexed to inflation/cost of living, and they increase to protect purchasing power.
2. **Defined Contribution Pension (DCP)**: With this type of plan, your benefit at retirement depends on how much is contributed. Your employer will contribute a specific amount, and you might be required to contribute a portion as well. Contributions made (by either you or the employer) are based on a fixed percentage of your income, or on a dollar amount. With a DCP, you usually have some input as to where the money is invested. You can influence how much you receive in the end by the investment choices you make. Group RRSPs and employee profit-sharing plans are types of DCPs, as are certain nonregistered plans that allow you to save money in an account other than RRSP.

According to the Alberta Federation of Labour, 60 percent of Canadian workers in the private sector don't have a private pension plan with their employers. According to information from the Fraser Institute, that number is different, with 24 percent of private sector employers covered by a registered pension plan in 2011, while 88.2 percent of public sector employers were covered.

This means that you aren't likely to be covered by a pension from your employer. Indeed, DBPs are quickly disappearing from the private sector; they are being replaced by retirement accounts that place more responsibility on individuals. Growth in pensions is often indexed to a particular set of investments, such as a bond index or a stock index, since money held in a pension account is often invested in a fund that tracks a particular index.

In some cases, if you have DBP, it's possible to receive a bridge pension. This is a pension option that provides you with an additional amount if you retire early. So, if your company offers bridging until you are sixty and you retire early at age fifty-five, you will receive an additional amount to your pension for those years, until you can start taking CPP benefits early. In some cases, you can use bridging until you are sixty-five. Check with your employer about the possibilities.

Survivors might also be able to receive benefits from an employer-sponsored pension. Make sure that you arrange your beneficiaries in a way that allows for your partner to receive some benefit. Realize, though, that in many cases the survivor benefit is less than the benefit you receive while you are alive.

When it's time to collect on your pension, you can decide on taking the pension, which amounts to receiving a life annuity, or you can commute it to a life income fund (LIF). If you are changing jobs, you can convert your pension to an annuity or to a LIF. Before you do that, though, make sure that you understand what a LIF entails.

What is a LIF?

A LIF is a way to receive a set amount of income during retirement. You can turn your pension into a LIF that can hold a number of assets, including GICs, mutual funds, and segregated funds. A LIF can give you more control over the investments that make up your retirement fund.

At the beginning of each year, you specify how much you will withdraw. Realize, though, that your decision is subject to minimum and maximum amounts. You will have to withdraw at least the minimum, and you cannot withdraw more than the maximum, since the point of a LIF is to provide you with income for the rest of your life.

You can also use your LIF as a way to protect your income from taxes, by adjusting the payments you receive. Modifying your withdrawal amounts can help you plan around OAS clawbacks and other tax issues that might arise.

If you have a LIRA or a locked-in RSP, a LIF can be a desirable option. You will have to decide on a LIF, LRIF, or life annuity if you have some sort of locked-in plan. A LIF can give you a little more flexibility than the other options—if flexibility is what you are looking for.

With a LIF, it's possible to name beneficiaries. Your spouse or common-law partner can be a beneficiary and roll the remaining amount into their RRSP with no tax consequences when you have a LIF.

THE NEW CANADIAN RETIREMENT

This is different from a pension, where your spouse/common-law partner might only receive between 40 percent and 60 percent of your benefit payout (depending on how you set up the pension) after your death. On top of that, many pension benefits stop paying out once your partner dies. With a LIF, it's possible for the assets to pass on to your children after both you and your partner are gone.

Don't forget that there might be other things to consider with a LIF. You might lose some of the health benefits that come with a pension when you convert your money into a LIF. You could also lose the bridge benefit that many pensions offer to help close the gap between early retirement and when you qualify for full CPP payments.

Additionally, you will need to determine what sort of return you need each year in order to match your pension income. If you will need an annual return of 8 percent or 9 percent in order to match your pension income, your LIF will probably need to be heavy on the equity funds. You will need to make sure that you have the risk tolerance to handle the situation. Run the calculations and make sure that choosing a LIF is the right move for you, since once you have made that decision, your money is pretty much "locked in"—unless you know how to get at it.

THE THREE SOURCES OF RETIREMENT INCOME

Life Income Fund (LIF) withdrawal percentages for 2014					
Age as at January 1, 2014*	Minimum withdrawal Percentage (non-qualified)	Maximum LIF withdrawal percentage for Ontario, New Brunswick, Saskatchewan & Newfoundland	Maximum LIF withdrawal percentage for Quebec, Manitoba, Nova Scotia & British Columbia	Maximum LIF withdrawal percentage for Alberta	Maximum LIF/RLIF withdrawal percentage for Federal (PBSA)
50	2.50%	6.27%	6.10%	6.51%	4.77%
51	2.56%	6.31%	6.10%	6.57%	4.80%
52	2.63%	6.35%	6.10%	6.63%	4.84%
53	2.70%	6.40%	6.10%	6.70%	4.89%
54	2.78%	6.45%	6.10%	6.77%	4.93%
55	2.86%	6.51%	6.40%	6.85%	4.98%
56	2.94%	6.57%	6.50%	6.94%	5.03%
57	3.03%	6.63%	6.50%	7.04%	5.09%
58	3.13%	6.70%	6.60%	7.14%	5.15%
59	3.23%	6.77%	6.70%	7.26%	5.22%
60	3.33%	6.85%	6.70%	7.38%	5.29%
61	3.45%	6.94%	6.80%	7.52%	5.38%
62	3.57%	7.04%	6.90%	7.67%	5.46%
63	3.70%	7.14%	7.00%	7.83%	5.56%
64	3.85%	7.26%	7.10%	8.02%	5.67%
65	4.00%	7.38%	7.20%	8.22%	5.78%
66	4.17%	7.52%	7.30%	8.45%	5.91%
67	4.35%	7.67%	7.40%	8.71%	6.06%
68	4.55%	7.83%	7.60%	9.00%	6.22%
69	4.76%	8.02%	7.70%	9.34%	6.40%
70	5.00%	8.22%	7.90%	9.71%	6.60%
71	7.38%	8.45%	8.10%	10.15%	6.83%
72	7.48%	8.71%	8.30%	10.66%	7.09%
73	7.59%	9.00%	8.50%	11.25%	7.39%
74	7.71%	9.34%	8.80%	11.96%	7.73%
75	7.85%	9.71%	9.10%	12.82%	8.14%
76	7.99%	10.15%	9.40%	13.87%	8.60%
77	8.15%	10.66%	9.80%	15.19%	9.13%
78	8.33%	11.25%	10.30%	16.90%	9.76%
79	8.53%	11.96%	10.80%	19.19%	10.50%
80	8.75%	12.82%	11.50%	22.40%	11.39%
81	8.99%	13.87%	12.10%	27.23%	12.47%
82	9.27%	15.19%	12.90%	35.29%	13.84%
83	9.58%	16.90%	13.80%	51.46%	15.59%
84	9.93%	19.19%	14.80%	100.00%	17.93%
85	10.33%	22.40%	16.00%	100.00%	21.20%
86	10.79%	27.23%	17.30%	100.00%	26.12%
87	11.33%	35.29%	18.90%	100.00%	34.33%
88	11.96%	51.46%	20.00%	100.00%	50.74%
89	12.71%	100.00%	20.00%	100.00%	100.00%
90	13.62%	100.00%	20.00%	100.00%	100.00%
91	14.73%	100.00%	20.00%	100.00%	100.00%
92	16.12%	100.00%	20.00%	100.00%	100.00%
93	17.92%	100.00%	20.00%	100.00%	100.00%
94 and above	20.00%	100.00%	20.00%	100.00%	100.00%

Unlocking your LIF

Once you put your money into a LIF, there are restrictions on how much you can take out each year. Your possible withdrawal amounts are bounded in terms of minimum and maximum by the Income Tax Act from each year. If you want to operate outside those bounds, you will need to "unlock" your LIF.

Options for unlocking your LIF are based on the rules set forth by the federal government, as well as by your provincial/territorial government.

Some of the options for unlocking your LIF include:

- **One-time 50 percent unlocking**: With this option, you are entitled to convert up to 50 percent of the total market value of your LIF holdings to a tax-deferred account after you reach age fifty-five. Saskatchewan is the one exception, and that province allows you to convert up to 100 percent of your assets. This is a one-time opportunity, so you won't be able to convert from your LIF to the same degree again.
- **Small balance unlocking**: If you have a small balance (and you are at least fifty-five), you can convert your account to your RRSP or RRIF. A small balance is one that amounts to less than 50 percent of that year's maximum pensionable earnings.
- **Financial hardship unlocking**: Canadians who can show that they have financial hardship can unlock some of their LIF money. You have to be able to show low income or show that you have costs related to a disability or to medical issues.
- **Shortened life expectancy unlocking**: If some sort of physical or mental condition is shortening your life expectancy, it's possible to

THE THREE SOURCES OF RETIREMENT INCOME

unlock the total value of your LIF. However, you need to have a doctor certify your shortened life expectancy.

- **Nonresident unlocking**: Another way to unlock your LIF is to move away. As long as you aren't employed by the organization that originated your pension funds, and as long as you have lived outside of Canada for at least two consecutive years, it's possible for you to unlock your entire LIF.

Make sure that you understand the realities of locked-in funds, no matter what kind of accounts they are. Once your money is locked in, it can be difficult to properly get at it later.

Pension vs. LIF

Most retirees have to make the choice between taking pension benefits or converting the pension to a LIF. In these cases, it's important that you carefully consider your options and determine what course of action will suit you best.

Some of the things to consider when it comes to deciding between a pension and a LIF include:

Income: The way you receive income differs between a pension and a LIF. With a pension, you receive a set amount of income. A formula is used to determine your benefits, and you receive a guaranteed amount each year. Your income can't be stopped, and you don't have to worry about it fluctuating with interest rates and changes in the stock market. However, unless you have a public sector plan, you aren't likely to see your income indexed to inflation.

A LIF, on the other hand, doesn't feature a set payout amount. You can adjust the amount you receive, as long as you stick to the given annual parameters. Income can also fluctuate if the value of the LIF changes along with the markets. Because LIFs are built with investments that have the potential to lose value, the income from your LIF might change over time.

Investment decisions: Because a pension defines a set amount for a payout, you don't have to worry about making investment decisions with your pension. The pension's investment decisions are made by others.

If you choose a LIF, you are responsible for the investment decisions. At the same time, though, you also have more flexibility. If the pension administrator miscalculates and something goes wrong, you could see a cut in payouts. With a LIF, you are in charge of your own retirement account destiny. You can include a variety of investments of your choosing, from the safety and stability of GICs to the higher earning potential of equity mutual funds and stocks.

For some, though, the idea of making investment decisions with a LIF is intimidating. But that's usually not a problem if you can get a little help from a trusted financial planner. He or she can guide you as you attempt to make the right decision for your situation and as you choose investments for your LIF.

Estate value: If you care about passing assets on to your children, a pension probably isn't going to work for you. A pension has almost no estate value. Your partner can continue receiving benefits from your pension (a reduced amount), but once your spouse or common-law partner passes on, the payments stop. Your children won't receive anything.

A LIF works differently. Upon the death of the account owner, the LIF reverts to the estate. Beneficiaries receive the assets remaining in the LIF without any "locking" restrictions. The assets in a LIF can pass on to your legal partner without extra tax consequences, and they can easily be rolled into a registered retirement plan. If your partner dies before you, it's possible to change the beneficiary information to pass the assets on to someone else, such as a child.

Tax planning: In general, a LIF is more flexible. This is true when it comes to tax planning as well. As long as you withdraw the minimum from your LIF, you can reduce your income if you want a better deal. Some retirees use the ability to modify LIF withdrawals to help them avoid clawbacks.

On the other hand, a pension can be split. You can assign pension credits to your legal partner, making it possible to take advantage of a strategy that has its own tax benefits.

Other flexibility: A LIF also has other flexibilities. Your LIF can be taken back to a LIRA or locked-in RRSP if you are under the age of seventy-one. Additionally, the money in your LIF is eligible as pension income after the age of sixty-five.

Make sure to carefully consider these options before making your decision.

Deferred Profit-Sharing Plan (DPSP)

Some employers offer a DPSP. With this type of plan, the employer makes contributions by sharing some of the profits that the company makes. Only an employer makes contributions to this type of plan. It's considered a type of employer-sponsored pension, and the money an employee receives in his or her account is not taxed until it is withdrawn.

Employers like these accounts because they are inexpensive, and the contributions made to employees' retirement accounts are fully deductible when tax time rolls around. Plus, employers can choose to take advantage of vesting requirements. If an employee leaves before the funds are totally vested, the money the employer contributed reverts back. Also, it's possible for the rules of the DPSP to insist that employees can't withdraw money while they are employed.

The flexibility offered by a DPSP makes it a very popular choice, especially since these profit-sharing plans can also be used in conjunction with group RRSPs that allow employees to contribute to their retirement futures as well.

For the employee, there is the advantage of receiving retirement help from the company and a tax-deferred retirement nest egg. Plus, it's possible at some point to roll a DPSP into your RRSP.

Severance packages

Another way that your employer can help you with retirement income is through a severance package. However, you need to carefully consider the way that you approach your severance package. The reality is that a package can come in the form of a large sum of taxable income. You want to do what you can to reduce the immediate impact of a severance package and try to avoid having taxes take a huge bite out of what you receive.

It's possible to roll over some or all of your severance to your RRSP. You don't need RRSP contribution room to do this. You can roll over $1,500 per year prior to 1989 and $2,000 per year up to 1995. This can be a great help if you are interested in boosting your retirement savings.

Once you have taken advantage of this provision, you can then decide to use your unused RRSP contribution room. Make a contribution with pretax amounts to improve your tax liability. Request a direct transfer to make sure that everything is handled properly and that your RRSP is properly funded with your severance money.

Another option is to ask for a deferred severance payment. With this strategy, you receive your severance amount over time, rather than all at once. By dividing it up among tax years, you can reduce your tax bill. Consult a knowledgeable financial planner or tax professional who can help you figure out how to best handle this situation.

Your remaining cash options, after you have used the other options and you still have money in your hands, can be maximized if you consider the following three options:

1. Top off your spouse's RRSP if there is room. You can use your RRSP contribution for your spouse, but your severance money can only be rolled directly into your own RRSP, so make sure you understand how the flow of money works to your best advantage.
2. Set up a flow-through limited partnership. This type of arrangement can provide you with tax deductions and provide a good way for you to reduce what you owe legally.
3. Reduce your nondeductible debt. Another good use of the money is to reduce debt. If the debt isn't tax-deductible, consider doing what you can to pay it down. The high interest you pay on such debt can destroy your peace of mind and negatively impact your finances.

Your company income action plan

Take a look at all of your sources of company income and create a plan based on what is likely to work best for you. Your pension decision is huge; you don't want to get it wrong. Consult with a retirement specialist to help you determine how to make everything work for you.

In today's low-rate environment, it can be hard to choose an annuity, since the payout isn't going to be as great. As a result, it can make sense to choose a flexible LIF for income and growth. You should also consider ways to increase the tax efficiency of a severance package and figure out how you can best utilize your DPSP.

Finally, you might decide to work for a little longer in order to avoid drawing on your retirement assets as much. Even a part-time job can make a difference in how long your retirement assets last.

Personal income

With company pensions changing, and with the government continuing to make changes to the way benefits are distributed, it's important that you focus on the aspects of your retirement income that you can control. This means you need to be on top of planning your own personal assets for income later on down the road.

You have a number of options when it comes to your retirement—including tax-advantaged options that can provide you with a way to more efficiently grow your assets over time.

THE THREE SOURCES OF RETIREMENT INCOME

Registered Retirement Savings Plan (RRSP)

The RRSP is the cornerstone of individual retirement planning in Canada. Your contributions to the RRSP are tax-deferred, meaning that you receive a tax deduction now. Since you make contributions with pre-tax dollars, your money grows more efficiently over time.

You can hold a number of different investments in your RRSP. Stocks, bonds, funds, GICs, and other assets can grow in your RRSP and provide you with a solid return over time. It's important to remember that the RRSP is a long-term retirement building strategy. You need to start as early as you can to contribute and contribute as much as possible.

It's a good idea to build your RRSP to last at least thirty years. Your withdrawals should also be carefully choreographed. Realize that you will need to pay taxes on your withdrawals from your RRSP later on. As a result, you will want to make sure that you integrate your RRSP income plan with the income you receive from OAS, CPP, and your company retirement income plan. All of this needs to be orchestrated in a way that allows you to take advantage of your assets without losing too much to taxes.

If you have a legal partner, you can use a spousal RRSP to increase the amount of money your household has in total. Even if your spouse isn't working outside the home, it's possible for you to make contributions to his or her RRSP. This increases your total contribution room.

Additionally, a spousal RRSP can allow you to plan matters so that all of the income for the household isn't in the hands of the spouse that earns more. Since you pay taxes separately, it makes sense to plan your household finances in a way that reduces your *overall* tax liability as a family.

With the new pension-splitting rules, it's important to note that spousal RRSPs can still be useful. Because income-splitting rules for RRSP accounts only take effect at age sixty-five—and only when the RRSP becomes RRIF income—there is an advantage to using spousal RRSPs. Because it's possible for you to access RRSP money early, a spousal RRSP can help. Anytime you plan to use your income before age sixty-five, a spousal RRSP will help you assign that income to the spouse in the lower tax bracket and save you money overall.

Creating income from your RRSP

When you are ready to begin taking money out of your RRSP, it's possible for you to engage in a few options. You can turn your RRSP into a registered retirement income fund (RRIF), convert it to an annuity that lasts until you are ninety, or convert it into a life annuity. It's also possible for you to move the assets in your RRSP (or even your RRIF) to nonregistered accounts. Carefully consider the options—and your situation—and consult with a knowledgeable financial planner. With the right plan, you can choose the option that is best for your particular situation.

RRIF

The RRIF is the most popular choice when it comes to converting your RRSP into income. The RRIF can provide both income and growth. Since it is an income fund, it can continue to grow as the investments in the account appreciate over time. On top of that, the RRIF is rather flexible.

Your RRIF provides you with the ability to make a lump sum withdrawal if you want. Additionally, you can change income amounts each year. As you age, or as circumstances change, you can make different withdrawal amounts, provided that they are at least the minimum amount. This minimum is set each year based on your age (although you can choose to have the minimum set based on your spouse or common-law partner's age).

You'll want to plan your RRIF withdrawals in conjunction with your other sources of income, since you won't want to run into problems later. The minimum withdrawal schedule starts at age seventy (currently 5 percent withdrawal) and goes up (someone who is ninety-three would need to withdraw a minimum of 19.92 percent). In many cases, it makes sense to draw down your retirement accounts in a specific order. A good financial planner or retirement specialist can help you figure out the best way to draw down your retirement accounts.

RRIFs are also popular because they make an easy transition for the RRSP. On top of that, your RRIF can be added to your estate. Unused balances revert to your estate and pass to your survivors. One of the most attractive qualities of the RRIF is that it's possible to pass the unused balance on to your surviving spouse without any serious tax consequences.

RRIFs are much more flexible than annuities, and they provide you (and your survivors) with more options.

Annuities

Some retirees prefer annuities, however. Even though they are less flexible, they are more predictable. With an annuity, you know that you will receive the payment each month like clockwork. The income doesn't change with market conditions. When you use the money in your RRSP to buy an annuity, the amount you have, plus how long you are expected to live, are calculations used to determine your payout. There are usually two options for annuities:

1. **Annuity to age ninety**: If you think that you will pass on before you reach the age of ninety, you can choose this option. You buy an annuity that pays out until you reach age ninety. The payments are usually a little higher with this option, since the company issuing the annuity knows that it will need to make payments only for a set period of time. If you live beyond ninety, though, you will need to have backup assets, since the annuity payments will stop.
2. **Life annuity**: For retirees who want to be assured that they will continue to receive annuity payments until they die, a life annuity can be an attractive choice. The payments with a life annuity are often a little smaller than those offered by a term annuity, since the company making the payouts has no idea when you will pass on. But, the income is guaranteed for life.

Before you choose an annuity, make sure that you carefully consider the implications. There are tax issues to be aware of, and you should realize that your surviving spouse or common-law partner might not receive payments after you die. In some cases there is a reduced benefit, depending on how the annuity is structured. Also be aware that some annuities are complex in structure, and there can be high fees. While annuities can be good choices for some retirees, you want to make sure that you fully understand all the terms and conditions that come with an annuity.

Should you defer your registered assets?

While registered plans can provide you with a way to save money for retirement, you should realize that deferring them is not always the way to go. Many retirees decide to put off dipping into their registered accounts and using registered assets. In the long run, though, this can be a poor decision.

Since your registered assets are tax-deferred, you will pay taxes on them later. If you move your RRSP assets into a RRIF, you become subject to a minimum withdrawal. This means that if your RRSP has done well, and you've deferred taking the assets, you will be *forced* to withdraw a specific amount each year, even if you don't need it, and even if it puts you in a higher tax bracket.

A higher tax bracket can be detrimental to your overall financial stability, and it can erode your real returns. On top of that, deferring your registered assets can also result in an OAS clawback, and that is never a desirable situation.

Finally, you want to consider the impact deferred registered assets can have on your spouse. If you die before your legal partner, this can put a large registered investment in the hands of your survivor, creating large taxation issues and resulting in OAS eligibility issues. You and your spouse need to coordinate your retirement income efforts and make choices about your accounts jointly. Get the help of a financial professional to learn the best way to go about ordering your withdrawals and coming up with a plan to avoid overtaxation and OAS problems.

Moving RRSP/RRIF assets to nonregistered accounts

It might seem counterintuitive to move your registered assets to nonregistered accounts, but in some cases it can be to your advantage. Here are some of the things to consider when converting at least some of your registered assets into nonregistered assets:

- **Asset/income splitting**: Once you start moving money around to different accounts, you can arrange ownership of the assets in a way that makes sense for your household. You can assign some of the assets to a lower-income partner so that the income is taxed at a lower rate.
- **Establish tax-efficient income**: Your planning with a nonregistered account can actually make you more tax efficient in the future. You can choose assets that are naturally tax efficient. It can also improve the tax efficiency for the spousal beneficiary, since you aren't dealing with the large registered investment at death. Consult a tax professional or financial planning professional for more information on using nonregistered assets to promote your overall tax efficiency in the future.
- **Lump sum withdrawals**: While it is possible to take lump sum withdrawals from certain registered accounts, it's not always easy, and the consequences can be disappointing. With a nonregistered account, it is a little easier to take those lump sum withdrawals without too much trouble.
- **Control over the assets**: With a nonregistered account, you are in total control over the assets. When you convert to an annuity, you lose control in a very real way. With the RRIF, you are forced to take minimum withdrawals. When you convert to a nonregistered account, you can choose when to withdraw, and how much you want to withdraw.
- **Estate**: It's also possible to take advantage of how user-friendly a nonregistered account is when it passes to your estate. It is more tax-friendly in many cases, and this can be an advantage to your survivors/heirs.

Consider moving some of your assets to nonregistered accounts as part of your overall retirement strategy, and you could reap the benefits.

Tax-Free Savings Account (TFSA)

One of the more recent offerings for long-term savings is the TFSA. With this account, you make contributions with pretax dollars. You won't receive a tax benefit for making contributions now, but your money will grow tax free. When you are ready to withdraw, you can do so without worrying about paying taxes. So, if taxes go up, or if you are in a higher tax bracket later, you save money on taxes because you have already paid at today's lower rates.

You can hold a number of different assets in your TFSA, including individual equities, funds, GICs, and other items. All of your earnings—no matter whether they are in the form of interest, capital gains, or dividends—grow tax free. So your increase isn't taxed at all.

Anyone who has reached the age of majority for his or her province and who has a Social Insurance Number can open a TFSA. If the age of majority in your province is nineteen, the good news is that you can carry your contribution room forward from age eighteen, so you can make extra contributions to make up for that "lost" year. There are no income requirements or restrictions when it comes to TFSA contributions.

The annual contribution limit is set each year and is indexed to inflation. Contribution room carries forward indefinitely, so you can get your full amount over time. For example, the current contribution limit in 2014 is $5,500. If you only contribute $4,500 this year, you have $1,000 of contribution room that carries forward. This means that you could contribute $6,000 next year and $6,000 the year after if you decide to split your unused contribution room into two payments. However you decide to use your unused contribution room is acceptable.

Another great thing about the TFSA is that it is very flexible. You can withdraw money at any time and make more contribution room later. So, if you contribute $5,500 throughout the year until November but then decide to withdraw $2,000 at the beginning of December, you have just created $2,000 of contribution room. You can replace that money in subsequent years, just as if you had never made the full contribution in the first place.

TFSAs also come with a number of other attractive benefits:

- **Survivor benefits**: Upon your death, the balance reverts to your surviving spouse tax-free. When the surviving spouse dies, the death balance passes on to the estate without tax.
- **Income isn't used for benefits**: The income from your TFSA is not used when testing for government benefits, so it won't affect your eligibility for OAS and other benefits.
- **Spousal contributions**: You can make contributions to your spouse's TFSA without attribution to the contributor.
- **Asset and income splitting**: It's possible to split your assets in a way that allows you to draw from your TFSA while preserving government benefits and tax credits.

Summary

Pay attention to your various sources of income for your retirement. Make sure you understand how each source works and where the money will come from. You also want to make sure that you understand the

THE THREE SOURCES OF RETIREMENT INCOME

tax consequences associated with each type of account and the different roles each of them play.

But you can't just focus on your own accounts. You also need to include your spouse or common-law partner's accounts as well. Your retirement income strategy needs to be based on your entire household's income sources.

Consider the best way to use your money, whether it's commuting or converting to an income fund of some sort, or whether it's making use of annuities. Don't forget that TFSAs can play an important role and that in some cases nonregistered accounts can add to your tax efficiency. Your strategy should include all the options; this means you will probably need help from a knowledgeable financial planner.

At this point, financial and tax planning is key. You need a strategy to improve your tax efficiency while maximizing your income. You will also need to ensure your income's longevity so that you don't outlive it.

CHAPTER FOUR:

TAXES ARE KEY

Tax planning is important

Developing an understanding of income taxes and how they apply to retirement income is extremely important. It's not necessary for every retiree to become an expert in taxation, but it is important to have a general idea of how taxes can impact your retirement future. You should have an idea of the basic tax laws that will affect your retirement income, and you should have an idea of what you can do to increase your tax efficiency so that your money lasts longer.

Improper tax planning during retirement is the single biggest hole in most retirement plans. Poor and inefficient tax planning can lead to diminished after-tax retirement income. Comprehensive tax planning, though, can significantly increase after-tax retirement income and ensure that all retirement assets are properly drawn on.

This step is one that many people miss. Too often, we believe that proper tax planning is more about improving tax efficiency during employment years. Too many people falsely believe that tax planning just doesn't matter as much during retirement, after they are no longer bringing earned income to the table. There is nothing further from the truth. Your income during retirement is still subject to taxation, and, what's more, it might be subject to greater taxation, depending on how well you have done for yourself. Without the proper tax planning, your retirement assets can be greatly diminished when the government comes to take its share.

Federal tax brackets

One of the first things you need to understand is that Canada has a progressive tax system. That means that as you earn more income, you will pay a larger percentage of it in taxes.

However, Canada also operates on a marginal tax rate system. This means that as you move up a tax bracket, the percentage that you pay only applies to the income within that bracket. You aren't taxed one rate on your entire income. Instead, your income is taxed on a tiered basis.

The table below illustrates the federal income tax brackets for (2014):

As you can see, if you make $136,000, you won't be taxed at a 29 percent rate on the entire amount. You will be taxed 29 percent on only $946 of that amount.

Federal tax rates for 2014

- 15% **on the first** $43,953 of taxable income, +
- 22% **on the next** $43,954 of taxable income (on the portion of taxable income over $43,953 up to $87,907), +
- 26% **on the next** $48,363 of taxable income (on the portion of taxable income over $87,907 up to $136,270), +
- 29% of taxable income **over** $136,270.

Understand that provincial and territorial tax rates also need to be considered. You will have to pay income taxes at a rate that is set by your provincial/territorial government on top of what you owe to the federal government.

Different income = different taxation

It's also important to understand that all income is not created equal. Different income is taxed differently. Some income, such as income from dividends, is treated differently than "regular" earned income. Understanding how this income is taxed is important as you begin making plans for how to fund your retirement.

Earned income: This is income that represents what you earn, as in a job. It's fully taxable as income, and it's what most people think of when they think of an income tax.

Interest income: If you receive income from certain sources, it is 100 percent taxable. This is income that you receive from interest yields on GICs, high-interest savings accounts, private loans made to others, and bonds. Any interest income that you receive is added to your "regular" income and taxed at your marginal tax rate. If you want to protect some of this income from maximum taxation, you can keep it in a tax-advantaged account. Because interest income can translate into high taxes, you can keep it in a RRSP in order to defer the taxes until you might be in a lower bracket. You can also keep some assets, like GICs, savings accounts, and bonds, in a TFSA. In that case, the earnings you receive are never taxed.

Capital gains income: When an asset you own appreciates in value, it is known as a capital gain. If you buy one hundred shares of a stock at twenty dollars a share, you have spent $2,000. Over time, you let that stock sit. Over the course of the next twenty-five years, the stock price increases to forty-five dollars a share. Now, your one hundred shares are worth $4,500. The difference between what you paid for the stock and what it is worth now is a capital gain of $2,500. When you sell that stock, you will pay taxes on that gain.

The good news is that capital gains have a preferred tax rate. You won't have to pay taxes on your gain at your fully taxable marginal tax rate. Instead, your gains are subject to a 50 percent inclusion rate. Only 50 percent of the profit is taxed at your marginal rate. So, in our example, $1,250 is added to your income and taxed at your marginal tax rate.

It is important to note that if you keep an investment in a registered account, like the RRSP, the gains are not taxed. However when you withdrawal money from your RRSP it is taxed 100% as income. In essence, your asset has grown tax-free but tax at 100% will still have to be paid on withdrawals.

It can make sense to keep your capital-appreciating assets outside of your RRSP for another reason: harvesting capital losses. The other side to the coin of a capital gain is a capital loss. You can use your capital losses to offset some of your capital gains. Let's say that you have your $2,500 gain from the stock in the example above. But you also sold another stock and realized a loss of $2,000. You can use your capital losses to offset your gains. In this case, your total profit, after you subtract your loss from your gain, is $500. The 50 percent inclusion rate applies only to your total capital gains profit, so you will add only $250 to your income to be taxed at your marginal tax rate.

You can further shelter your capital gains by keeping your capital assets in a TFSA; when you withdraw money from a TFSA, it is not taxed.

Dividend income: Some companies are willing to pay a portion of their profits to shareholders. These payments are known as dividends. Often, corporations pay dividends on a quarterly basis. Dividend distributions are "extra" payments, and they come on top of any capital appreciation you might see.

Dividend income is particularly tax efficient. Distributions are made after the company has already paid taxes. So, you receive an enhanced dividend tax credit on dividend payments from Canadian public companies after you have figured your dividend tax.

When figuring your tax situation based on dividends from Canadian companies, you start out by "grossing up" your dividends received. The amount you gross up depends on the year. For 2014, eligible dividends are grossed up by 38 percent. The grossed up amount is then added to your income for the year. So, if you receive $1,500 in dividends for the year, you gross up the amount you owe by 38 percent, which in this case is $570. Add that amount to the dividends you received, and the total you add to your income is $2,070. That amount is part of your marginal tax rate.

But, you do get a tax credit to help offset some of that amount. You will receive a federal tax credit and a provincial/territorial tax credit. In our example, let's say your marginal rate is 26 percent. So, you will multiply your grossed up dividends by that number to get $538.20. That's how much tax you owe.

Now, though, you can figure out how much you will actually have to pay. You will get a tax credit from the federal government amounting to 15.0198 percent of your grossed up dividends, so you multiply that by the $2,070 to get $310.91. You then subtract that credit amount from what you owe ($538.20 - $310.9) to come up with $227.30 owed in federal taxes. You can also subtract the credit for your province or territory to further reduce the tax you owe on dividends.

Understand that dividends received from foreign companies are 100 percent taxable; you won't receive this preferential tax treatment. Additionally, there might be other issues, such as an effect on your OAS payouts or the requirement to pay the alternative minimum tax. Consult a financial planner for help with sorting through these issues.

Fully taxable income from other sources: Other income is fully taxable. This includes payments from OAS, CPP, LIF, RRSP/RRIF, and all rental income. You will need to be able to balance the taxes you owe on these sources of income with preferred income sources that come with tax advantages.

Tax-exempt income: Some income is actually exempt from taxes. When you receive an injury award (such as winning a lawsuit), lottery winnings, inheritances, gifts, and life insurance proceeds, you do not have to pay taxes on the income.

Managing your net income figure

One of the best things you can do for your retirement is to manage your income with an eye toward proper tax planning. Think about what your taxes will look like later on in life, during retirement, and not just how they affect you right now.

Remember that you will likely have income from a variety of sources—and many of them will be fully taxable. Considering which assets to hold in different accounts can be an important part of your retirement planning. If you invest in eligible companies that pay dividends, it can make sense to avoid holding those investments in your RRSP. You will essentially mitigate the value of the special advantages that come with eligible dividends.

While the particulars of your own situation might differ, depending on your province or territory, and while things might change depending on the way marginal tax rates are adjusted over time, you can still get an idea of how important it is to plan your income carefully as you approach retirement.

As you can see, the most desirable situation is to have eligible dividend income. It is the most tax efficient. The least tax efficient is interest income, which is fully taxable. One of the best things you can do now is to plan out your assets for retirement and keep the least-tax-efficient investments in your TFSA or even your RRSP. Don't take up contribution dollars for these accounts by holding already-efficient assets in registered accounts.

In addition to having a strategy for building up your nest egg, you will want a strategy for drawing down your nest egg in the most effective manner possible. Work with a knowledgeable financial planner to decide in which order you should draw down your accounts, what types of accounts you should convert your pensions to, and what you should do with the money in your RRSP or other registered accounts.

You don't want to leave all of your registered accounts for last, since that could lead to a serious tax issue later. Instead, create an income strategy that takes into account all of your accounts and the accounts of your spouse or common-law partner. A solid income strategy, along with proper coordination, is vital if you want to live comfortably without overpaying in taxes during your retirement.

Use deductions and credits to increase your tax efficiency

Deductions and credits can increase your tax efficiency, reducing the amount of money you end up paying to the government. It's important to realize that you shouldn't *avoid* taxes or do anything illegal. You can, however, do everything you can legally to reduce what you owe. There's no sense in letting the government have more than it's entitled to.

There are plenty of strategies you can follow to help you reduce your tax liability. Just paying attention to where you keep your money can be a big help, as you can see above. Choosing tax-efficient investments and paying attention to the way different types of income are taxed can help you reduce what you owe while still allowing you to maintain your quality of life.

Among the ways to reduce your tax liability is to take advantage of tax deductions and tax credits. Tax deductions are designed to help you reduce your income. Because the amount of tax you pay is based upon your income, having a lower income can result in lower taxes. On the other hand, a tax credit is designed to directly reduce the amount of tax you owe. A tax credit basically acts as a gift card. After your tax has been figured out, the credit is applied to what you owe and directly reduces your liability, dollar for dollar. In general, a tax credit is more valuable than a tax deduction.

There are a couple of notable tax credits of interest to retirees:

1. **Age amount**: If you are sixty-five or older and you meet certain income requirements, you are eligible for an age amount tax credit. The income amount associated with this tax credit adjusts with

inflation, and the full amount that you are eligible for phases out as your income increases. If you have a low to modest income, though, you can reduce your tax liability in retirement with this credit.

2. **Pension income amount**: When you report pension (or annuity) income, or even superannuation or annuity payments, you might be eligible for a credit of up to $2,000. Make sure you understand the eligibility requirements before claiming this credit.

Understanding what you are entitled to is an important part of managing your income and your taxes during retirement.

Tax efficiency is an area where serious income improvements can be made. You should look especially hard for tax credits available to you after age sixty-five, since tax credits become fewer and farther between as you get older. You lose the credits that helped you while you were raising children, and your income from almost all of your retirement accounts—from pensions to registered retirement accounts—is 100 percent taxable.

With the help of tax planning, you can keep your net income low to help you in other areas. Not only will you owe less in taxes, but you can also preserve your access to government entitlements. Your OAS payments can be reduced if your income rises too high, and a little proper tax planning can help you avoid that issue.

Where and when to draw your assets

One of the most important aspects of tax planning is understanding where and when to draw your assets. As you consider where to keep your assets and which accounts to draw down first, keep in mind the tax rates.

Understanding where you are likely to stand in retirement is vital if you want to avoid losing some of your income to taxes.

It's tempting to put off drawing down your registered accounts and start with your other accounts. However, realize that you might actually just be putting yourself into a higher tax bracket. When you get to a certain point with some registered assets, you are *required* to withdraw a minimum amount each year. This means that you are forced to take income at a level that might put you in a higher tax bracket if you put off drawing down your registered assets.

Also, don't forget the TFSA. It's a relatively new development, but it has great potential value. You can put money into it and avoid taxes later; this is especially important if you believe that taxes will rise later. Carefully plan out (with the help of a knowledgeable adviser) which accounts to use and which to draw down first.

You want your retirement plan to have fully taxable income at lower rates, combined with tax-efficient income at higher rates. That way you are more likely to receive the maximum after-tax cash flow you need to live comfortably.

The taxman is waiting

It seems as though putting money into a tax-deferred account is a great idea right now. And it can be a good strategy to put money into a tax-deferred account at present. However, it's important to remember that eventually the tax man will be waiting. You will have to pay taxes, and the money is taxable after you withdraw the minimum.

When you withdraw money from your RRIF (usually converted from your RRSP), you are subject to minimums:

RRIF Minimum Withdrawal

Age at Start of Year	RRIFs set up after the end of 1992*	Age at Start of Year	RRIFs set up after the end of 1992*
65	4.00%	80	8.75%
66	4.17%	81	8.99%
67	4.35%	82	9.27%
68	4.55%	83	9.58%
69	4.76%	84	9.93%
70	5.00%	85	10.33%
71	7.38%	86	10.79%
72	7.48%	87	11.33%
73	7.59%	88	11.96%
74	7.71%	89	12.71%
75	7.85%	90	13.62%
76	7.99%	91	14.73%
77	8.15%	92	16.12%
78	8.33%	93	17.92%
79	8.53%	94+	20.00%

Money that you withdraw from your various registered accounts is fully taxable. Also, don't forget that some of the money you withdraw will be subject to withholding taxes once you reach your minimum annual withdrawal:

You don't want to find yourself waiting too long to withdraw from registered assets. Since annual minimums, whether it's for a LIF or a RRIF or some other account, are figured based on the assets in the account, your minimums—if you have let the account grow to be quite large over time—can put you into a higher tax bracket. You might also see your immediate cash flow impacted by the withholding amount if you have exhausted other options.

It's important to put together a withdrawal plan that helps you avoid problems come tax time. This means that you need to consider your withdrawal rate over the course of your entire retirement, and not just when you reach the point where you have to take minimum withdrawals from registered accounts.

You will need to carefully orchestrate your entire withdrawal strategy throughout your retirement, including your partner's accounts and income.

The three keys to efficient tax planning

As you plan your retirement income to be as tax efficient as possible, keep in mind the three keys to efficient tax planning:

1. Deduct

Your first move is to deduct what you can, when you can deduct it. Before you retire, use RRSP or RPP contributions to help you invest at a lower tax bracket now.

Other ways to get tax deductions include interest expenses from qualifying loans. Check with a knowledgeable tax planner to find out what deductions you are eligible for throughout your career and how you can reduce your tax liability.

Getting into a lower tax bracket now so that you pay lower taxes at this point in your career can improve your efficiency overall.

Don't forget to look at credits as well. And keep looking for special deductions and credits even after you retire. But you will have more luck with a great number of deductions and credits prior to retirement. Take advantage of them while you can.

You can use tax-efficient investments, like eligible dividends, to receive further benefits due to the assets you choose.

2. Divide

You can also divide your income. It doesn't just have to be about your own income if you have a spouse or a common-law partner—particularly if your partner makes less than you do.

You can use spousal RRSP contributions and jointly held property to reduce your assets, as well as reduce your tax liability. Since your partner is taxed separately, you can shift some of the assets in your name to your partner's so you can be taxed at a lower rate. In many cases, this division of assets results in lower overall taxation for your household.

3. Defer

Deferring taxation is beneficial as it leaves more money with you longer, rather than reducing it as you go. Your RRSP, RPP and cash value life insurance are all ways to defer what you pay in taxes now to a later time.

However, you can't just defer your taxes and expect everything to work out. Any deferment has to be a part of your overall retirement plan. You need to plan ahead, understanding fully how to adjust your income in retirement to avoid making the deferment even worse for you in terms of taxes later on.

Pension splitting

During retirement, one of the best tax strategies you have available to you is pension splitting. With pension splitting, you can give up 50 percent of your eligible pension income to your spouse. This is something that is done solely for tax purposes. You don't have to transfer any actual assets to your spouse in order for pension splitting to work. The split/transfer of pension payments is completed entirely on paper when you file your tax returns.

You do have to make sure that your pension plan is eligible for splitting. A registered pension plan—whether it's a defined benefit plan or a defined contribution plan—is eligible. Most of the time, the registered plan you have through work is eligible.

Even if you don't have a pension plan through work, it's still possible to engage in pension splitting by converting your RRSP to a RRIF or a life annuity. However, you can't make this conversion until you are sixty-five, so you are at a bit of a disadvantage if you don't have a registered pension plan through work.

Realize that income from your OAS is not eligible for splitting. Your CPP can be split, but it's not simply a matter of taking care of it through your tax return. You actually have to apply to split your CPP.

Eligibility for pension splitting

Before you engage in this tax strategy, make sure you qualify. In addition to having eligible pension income, you also need to meet the following conditions:

- You must be married or be in a common-law partnership in the year for which you want to split the pension income. Additionally, you can't have lived apart for more than ninety days due to marriage/partnership issues.
- You and your partner must both be residents of Canada on December 31 of the year in which you want to split your income.

It's also possible to take advantage of the pension credit as part of your splitting efforts. If you qualify for the pension credit, you can get $2,000 tax-free. You can also assign $2,000 to your spouse/common-law partner, and he or she can receive the credit as well (if eligible). Effectively, that means you get $4,000 tax-free from your pension with the help of the credit plus pension splitting. However, this is done on a per-person basis. If your partner has his or her own pension income, that income has to be used for tax credit purposes first.

Pension splitting can be a way to bring down the overall tax liability of your household. If your higher income puts you in the 28 percent tax bracket, but your partner is only in the 15 percent tax bracket, you can shift some of your pension income to your partner. This can move you down a bracket, and your combined tax liability overall might be less than your individual liability. This strategy can reduce your total household tax payment.

Summary

We must all pay taxes; it's the way that we pay for the services we enjoy as a society. However, there is no reason to pay more than you have to. And there is certainly no reason to overpay when you are retired and living on an income that might be reduced.

If you want to improve the chances that you will not outlive your money, you must pay attention to taxes. As you structure your retirement plan, make sure you understand how different assets and different types of income are taxed. Understand which assets come with tax efficiencies and which should be held in retirement accounts.

TAXES ARE KEY

Examine your choices so that you know which assets to use and when to use them. Understand which assets are best to defer. Finally, make sure that you understand the best way to combine your income so it is most efficient. A good tax professional or financial planner can help you identify the best way to structure you portfolio as well as suggest ways to most effectively draw down your assets during retirement.

Don't forget your spouse or common-law partner. Splitting your income can be a very tax-efficient strategy. Additionally, you don't want to increase your household tax bill by neglecting to plan for your spouse's income. Be vigilant when it comes to avoiding tax waste and make it a point to plan ahead so that you aren't seeing your retirement dreams eroded by paying unnecessary taxes.

CHAPTER FIVE:

FIVE TAX-SMART STRATEGIES THAT WILL SERVE YOU WELL

Reduce your tax liability

Now that you know how important tax planning is when it comes to building your wealth, you need to make an effort to use strategies that will benefit you over time.

By utilizing the following five tax-planning strategies throughout your life, and especially during your retirement, you can reduce your tax liability and keep more of your hard-earned cash.

1. Use a "buy and hold" strategy to defer paying taxes

One of the most effective ways to defer your taxes is to take a "buy and hold" approach to investing. The idea behind deferral is to put off paying taxes by making investment purchases and then holding on to them, rather than selling and realizing capital gains.

Deferring your taxes on investment gains can serve your interests in two different ways:

1. You keep more of your money now, and it is put to work on your behalf. Instead of paying taxes, your money stays in your investment account, and that means that you have the potential for greater gains on that money. The more money you have working on your behalf, the better compound growth works on your behalf.
2. When you do pay taxes, there is a good chance that you will be in a lower tax bracket. Many (but not all) retirees have a lower taxable income than they had while they were working, so putting off taxes until you have a lower income can help you save money in tax obligations.

For the most part, buy and hold is about controlling your asset turnover—especially on equity investments. This is a strategy used by **Mercer Private Counsel**. While we are far from perfect, our investment strategy has been quite successful over the years. Our strategy is to look for fundamentally sound investments that are likely to have staying power. Then, instead of trading frequently, we hold on to these investments.

Investments with strong fundamentals are likely to weather stock market storms and eventually generate significant growth. Choose these types of investments, and you will be more likely to see long-term success.

And that's the point. You want to choose investments that keep you from the need to trade frequently.

How should you invest?

You should consider a professionally managed portfolio, getting help from a portfolio manager who understands the principles of investing and who understands what you trying to accomplish. In some cases, this can provide you with an advantage over mutual funds. You can give the manager specific guidelines regarding your portfolio and the manager will handle the portfolio on a discretionary basis, based on, agreed upon criteria.

Realize, too, that buy and hold doesn't mean that you make a purchase and hang on to it forever. At times, prudent portfolio management requires you to make a few changes to keep your asset allocation in line. Your portfolio manager will periodically review your portfolio and make sure that the assets match your current risk tolerance and goals.

While you will eventually have to pay taxes on your investment gains, finding ways to put it off can be a big help down the road. Find ways to defer actually "locking in" your gain for as long as possible. It's the next best thing to a tax deduction.

2. Get your accountant and investment advisor working for you

Too often, we compartmentalize different aspects of our lives. This is also true of our finances. It's easy to keep your accountant separate from your investment advisor. However, if you want to make sure that you are getting the best possible tax deal, you need to make sure that your accountant and your investment advisor are on the same page.

If you want your wealth the most effectively managed, both your accountant and your investment advisor need a complete picture of your finances. This is about more than just sharing all of your information with both professionals. You also need to encourage your accountant and investment advisor to work together as part of your wealth management team.

Remember that all aspects of finances are entwined. Your financial plan needs to include investments, and it needs to consider the tax implications of the investments that you have and the accounts that you use. Your accountant and investment advisor can work together in order to integrate various aspects of your financial and estate plan.

Tax planning should be taking place year round, and not just in the spring. In fact, if you do your tax planning at the last minute, you are likely to miss out on a number of benefits that you would have had—if only you had taken advantage of them during the tax year. The biggest expenditure you are likely to make over the course of your lifetime is the payment of income tax. You don't want that to go wrong and with your accountant and your investment advisor working together, can help you avoid pitfalls.

Investment tax planning should be completed prior to the end of the calendar year. By the time your accountant, working independently of a financial advisor or investment advisor, looks over your tax information, it's usually too late for planning. Instead, get in the habit of always thinking of ways to reduce your taxes. When you have a wealth management team on your side, this can be a real help. Your investment advisor can provide information to your accountant, and the accountant can make good suggestions about how to proceed in order to reduce your tax bill.

It's especially important to remember that your ultimate goal should include a focus on after-tax returns. You might be surprised at how often the highest gross pretax return doesn't actually provide the most tax-advantaged results. If you aren't careful, you could see a higher gross return but see lower real returns after taxes are accounted for.

Rather than be unpleasantly surprised, do what you can to get your accountant and your investment advisor together. With the right strategy, you can see higher after-tax (or "real") returns, even if the gross returns are a little smaller than you would like.

3. Invest to beat inflation

Inflation is the almost-silent creeper. Few of us think about the impact of inflation on the future, but the reality is that inflation can devastate your retirement portfolio.

Inflation is the term that reflects the increase in the cost of living over time. Basically, as the years go by, your purchasing power decreases. Your dollar no longer buys as much as it used to. As the cost of living increases, you need to find a way to boost your income to preserve your purchasing power as much as you can.

Below is a good example of how your purchasing power can be eroded:

You buy a GIC at 3 percent for a fixed period of time. Let's say that you are in the top marginal bracket. If you are taxed at 50 percent, that means that your return after taxes is actually 1.5 percent. But wait: during this time inflation has been taking its toll. If inflation is at 2.5 percent, you actually see negative returns. Your after-tax return of 1.5 percent is less than the rate of inflation. Your real return is –1.0 percent. Even though your money is in a GIC, and earning an annual return, your true rate of return is negative, meaning that you lose money in real terms.

As you can see, retirees who are risk averse run the risk of losing money due to inflation. If you are concerned about so-called riskier investments, you will likely never be able to build the wealth you need to retire.

Beating inflation can be difficult, since, as a retiree, you might no longer be bringing in earned income. Instead, you have to rely on the income produced by your retirement portfolio. And, since retirees are living longer than ever, there is more time for inflation to go to work on your portfolio.

While it's not always easy to stay ahead of inflation and preserve your purchasing power, it is possible. Here are three successful steps you can take to fight inflation and maintain your purchasing power:

1. Dividend paying equities: Dividend stocks can help your portfolio because they provide regular income. For the best long-term results, it makes sense to purchase shares from legitimate blue chip companies. You can also use DRIPs to boost your investments and earnings.
2. Real-return bonds: These are bonds that adjust with the rate of inflation. You can use these securities to keep pace with what's happening in terms of inflation. This can be one way to preserve capital and invest without taking on a great deal of risk. However, even these probably aren't enough for you to build the kind of nest egg that allows you to retire comfortably.
3. Hard assets: You can also consider hard assets. These are assets that are more tangible. Hard assets include real estate and commodities. Gold is also a hard asset. In many cases, the US dollar moves inversely to hard assets, and this can reduce your risk due to inflation.

Consider your risk tolerance, and then choose the strategy (or use a combination of strategies) that works best for you and your family.

4. Replace your mutual funds with your own managed account

Rather than leave your retirement fate to mutual fund performance, you can consider creating your own "fund" through a managed account. A managed account can provide you with just what you need to improve your retirement account's performance over time—and save you money.

Mutual funds can get expensive

An actively managed mutual fund—one that requires a professional to manage the fund according to certain criteria—often costs a great deal more than you might expect. On top of that, it's important to understand that managed mutual funds can result in other costs, related to investment turnover within the fund.

While it can be comforting to know that a mutual fund is overseen by an "expert," the reality is that the mutual fund is expensive, and you can never be sure that the fund will be managed according to your long-term retirement interests. The fund manager is not beholden to you or any one person; instead, the manager works on behalf of the goals of the fund. You need to make sure that the fund in question is compatible with your goals before you invest your money.

A managed mutual fund often has a management expense ratio (MER) of about 2 to 2.5 percent. On the other hand, if you hire a qualified Portfolio Manager to help you invest, you might only pay a fee of 1.50 percent. That's a savings of approximately 0.75 percent every year.

That doesn't seem like much at first, but consider how it could impact your real returns. First of all, for every $100,000 you have invested in a managed account versus a managed mutual fund, you save $750 a year. Next, you have to consider what you could have done with those yearly savings. If you invest $750 a year, compounding at 8 percent for thirty years, that $750 becomes $85,000. Does that 0.75 percent difference seem so small now?

When you manage your portfolio with the help of your own dedicated professional, you have the opportunity to ensure that your portfolio is managed according to your individual requirements. You can give your portfolio manager directions about how to manage your retirement investments in a way that most benefits you. With a mutual fund, you have to be content with the parameters set by the fund. When you have your own portfolio managed by a professional in your pay, you can set your own parameters.

Not only can you see big savings over time with your own managed portfolio, but there might also be further benefits to eschewing managed mutual funds for your own creation. If you keep your retirement investment portfolio in a nonregistered account, you might be able to write off the management fee as an investment expense. This provides you with further after-tax savings that can aid you in your quest to make your retirement as tax efficient as possible.

Creating your own personal retirement portfolio

When you create your own personal retirement portfolio, you are, in essence, creating an individualized mutual fund. Your portfolio is assembled using investments that are designed to complement each other as they help you reach your wealth goals.

In order to put your retirement portfolio together, you should look for a qualified portfolio manager. Check the credentials of potential managers prior to committing your money. Sit down and spend time discussing your needs. Many managers are willing to talk with you for half an hour or an hour to assess your needs and provide you with a few recommendations. Remember you are seeking a professional with experience, integrity, credentials and a long-term track record.

Once you have a portfolio manager selected, get his or her help choosing investments for your fund. You will normally need at least $100,000 to follow this course of action, especially since you will need enough capital for your manager to assemble the investments required to help you meet your retirement income goals.

This strategy can provide you with peace of mind as well as result in a huge savings in terms of fees. On top of that, you can increase the performance potential of your portfolio with the help of a knowledgeable manager who can tailor the included investments to your specific situation.

5. Reduce capital gains by using capital losses

Finally, as you work to improve your portfolio's tax efficiency, don't forget that you can sell some of your investments at a loss in order to offset some of your capital gains.

A capital gain occurs when you sell an investment at a profit. If you buy one hundred shares of company X at fifty dollars a share (spending a total of $5,000) and decide to sell those shares later, when the price is seventy-five dollars a share, you will receive a total of $7,500. The difference is your capital gain. In this case, your gain is $2,500.

On the other hand, if you lose money on your investment transaction, you experience a capital loss. If you purchase one hundred shares of company Y at twenty-five dollars a share (spending $2,500), and sell at fifteen dollars a share (for a total of $1,500), you have a capital loss of $1,000.

It's true that capital gains are already reasonably tax efficient. However, your tax strategy shouldn't stop with the acknowledgement of capital gains and losses. Your gains will be taxed at a favorable rate, but you still pay taxes on the gains nonetheless. You can reduce your tax liability by selling a losing stock to offset your gains.

As you pursue this strategy, you should consult with your investment manager and your accountant in order to arrange the most advantageous situation for selling your investments. Here are two steps to follow as you prepare to sell investments for gains:

1. Put off the sale until the New Year.

Your first step is to put off the sale of a winning stock or fund until after the New Year if you are approaching year-end. It's true that you might need to sell some stocks earlier in the year, but if the year is drawing to a close, see if you can delay the sale.

When you put off the sale so that the final trade date falls in the following year, the gain is taxable in the next year. You basically have a year-long deferral of your taxes, and you also have more time to offset that gain with capital losses.

2. Sell losing stocks to offset your capital gains.

No matter what time of year you sell a winning stock, you should consider how you can offset those gains—reducing your investment income—with capital losses. In the example above, the sale of company X results in a gain of $2,500. However, the sale of company Y results in a loss of $1,000. You can then use that loss of $1,000 to offset the gains of $2,500. Instead of being taxed on a gain of $2,500, the sale of the losing stock reduces the amount of the gain to $1,500. You are taxed on only that $1,500, rather than on a larger amount.

Be careful, though. You should only sell a stock or a fund that you had planned to sell eventually, or one that has experienced a fundamental change. Don't sell an investment that is currently undervalued just to offset a gain (an undervalued investment should be held on to—provided it is still fundamentally sound).

Also, keep in mind that neither you, nor your spouse, can repurchase the investment within thirty days before or after the sale of the old investment. If you sell a losing investment only to repurchase it within thirty days at a "bargain," you will not be able to use the sale of the losing investment to offset your capital gains for tax purposes.

With the proper planning, and with help from qualified professionals, you can create a plan to provide yourself with the income you need in retirement while reducing your tax liability, and possibly unburdening a few investments that no longer suit your needs.

CHAPTER SIX:

LONG-TERM CARE: RETIREMENT PLAN KILLER

What's killing your retirement?

You might not be aware of it, but there is a lurking danger to your retirement plan. This danger is seen in the form of the need for long-term care. We don't like to think about our impending mortality—nor do we like to consider the reality that eventually we will lose our faculties.

When you are no longer able to care for yourself, you will need help. As boomers retire, they need more care. Eventually the care will have a significant impact on the need for more income, and eventually the estate.

Currently, 25 percent of women and 45 percent of men over the age of eighty-five live in long-term care institutions. The current average stay in a subsidized nursing care facility is about three years. The reality is that if you live to the age of eighty-five, chances are that you will spend some time in a nursing facility of some type.

Next, consider the cost of such facilities. Costs can easily run into the $200,000 range, depending on the level of care you need and how long you are in a facility. While it's not a cheering prospect to think on, it's one you need to consider. Long-term care can kill the best-laid retirement plans.

Instead of being surprised by the costs of long-term care, you need to plan ahead. You can use long-term care insurance and universal life insurance to help you reduce the impact of long-term care to your income, as well as use universal life insurance to protect the assets associated with your estate.

Long-term care insurance

Long-term care insurance can be a great help for the retiree who needs care and attention as age sets in. Long-term care insurance can cover the out-of-pocket expenses for a nursing home or for in-home care.

The great thing about the flexibility of long-term care insurance is that you can, to some extent, choose how you will be cared for. If you need help with some daily tasks, such as bathing or dressing, but you aren't quite ready to enter a nursing facility, your long-term care policy can cover the costs associated with having in-home help. Eventually, when you get to the point that you prefer the peace of mind that comes with having attendants available at any time, you can move to a nursing facility, and the long-term care coverage will kick in.

Who is eligible for a long-term care insurance policy?

In most cases, you are most likely to receive approval for a long-term care policy if you are a little younger. The insurance company will want to know your current health before issuing a policy. You will probably be subject to a physical exam and your age is important. Additionally, you will be tested on your cognitive health.

A complete medical history might be sought by the insurance company. You will need to share the frequency of your doctor visits, as well as divulge what medications you take and how frequently you take them. Your family history and your current state of independence will also be assessed.

Most insurance companies want to make sure that you have some years of paying premiums before a payout is needed. Insurance companies cover the costs associated with your long-term care by taking your premium payments and investing them. Companies want to know that they stand a decent chance of making enough from your premiums and the subsequent investments to cover the cost of your care—and make a profit as well.

As a result, if you are already in poor health, you probably won't receive a policy. If you are already in a nursing facility, or if you already need in-home help, you will likely be denied. On top of that, few applicants who are over the age of eighty receive approval for a long-term care insurance policy.

Indeed, you are better off applying for a policy while you are relatively young and comparatively healthy. Apply for long-term care insurance in your late fifties and sixties, while you are still active and fairly healthy, and you will more likely be approved for the policy, as well as pay reasonable premiums.

How are long-term care insurance premiums set?

Your long-term care premiums are set according to a number of factors. The insurance company will take into account your age and health, as well as your family history. If you are fairly young, and if you are in good health, you will probably pay lower premiums.

Your gender also plays a role in your long-term care insurance premium. If you are a woman, you will probably pay a higher premium—no matter your age and health. This is because the life expectancy for women is higher than it is for men. As a result, the expectation is that once women do need long-term care, they will need it for longer.

And, of course, your premium will take into account how much coverage you want. The more coverage you request, the higher the premium will be. The coverage you want will be considered along with your current age and health, and actuarial tables will be consulted to determine the likelihood that you will spend a long time in a care facility or need in-home help. If you want a high amount of coverage, and the estimate is that you will need a great deal of long-term help, your premium will be higher.

Also realize that many insurance policies increase as you age. Your long-term care insurance premium will probably not remain the same throughout the time you have it. As you enter your sixties and seventies, your premium will increase. Make sure that you plan for this premium increase as you age and make sure that you have adequate income to cover this increase.

So what happens if you pass on without ever needing the help of your long-term care policy? The good news is that your estate need not be diminished by the premiums you have paid. Some policies have a rider that allows for a "return of premium." This means that all of the money you have paid into the policy is returned if you haven't received any payouts to help you cover the cost of long-term care. However, even with this rider, you will still have to meet certain criteria for your estate to receive back the premiums you paid. Normally, you will have had to pay into the policy for at least five years for the rider to apply.

When do you receive payouts?

If you have purchased long-term care insurance, you need to pay attention to when you can start receiving your payouts. You don't receive the money for the asking. You have to meet certain conditions. Normally, you have to be incapable of performing two daily tasks without help. So, if you can no longer bathe and can no longer feed yourself, then those qualify as two daily living activities.

Before the insurance company starts making payments, your situation will need to be verified by a doctor. A doctor will come and observe your abilities and then certify to the insurance company that you need long-term care. Once that is taken care of, you can begin receiving payouts.

However, you should be aware that the payouts may not be enough to completely cover the cost of your care, depending on the type of care you receive. The payout you receive is based on the policy you purchased, which usually stipulates an amount of coverage per day. Many nursing facilities and in-home caregivers charge on a daily basis. For instance, the cost of a nursing facility might be $150 a day. If your insurance policy only covers $100 a day, then you will need to come up with the extra fifty dollars on your own, from your retirement savings.

Realize, too, that if you opt for in-home care, your insurance will only cover you for services rendered related to your care. You might not receive enough money to cover the cost of purchasing food or costs related to the maintenance and upkeep of your home. It's important that you take this into consideration as you plan ahead.

Before you settle on an insurance policy, it makes sense to do a little research. Look into the nursing care facilities that you might consider being admitted to. You might consider assisted living communities as well and see whether or not you can get a policy that covers those facilities. Find out what, exactly, is covered by the policy and how much you will need to pay in order to receive more coverage care. Be realistic as you shop for long-term care coverage and be prepared for it to cost more than you thought.

However, even though long-term care insurance can be expensive, it is still often better than the alternative—draining your retirement account and your estate's assets completely as you spend years in a nursing care facility. The need for long-term care can severely impact your retirement assets, and it will only become more expensive as retirees live longer.

If you can afford long-term care insurance, it can be a great product. Consider buying early on in your retirement and making the payment of premiums a priority. That way, when you do need help taking care of yourself, your policy will be waiting for you.

Universal life insurance

Another way you can protect your assets as you age, as well as gain a reasonably safe investment, is to purchase universal life insurance. Universal life insurance is life insurance for the next generation. It builds cash value that can be leveraged during your lifetime, and it can also be a great help in protecting your estate after you pass on.

Universal life insurance provides you with a way to invest in a tax-deferred way while providing a death benefit for your survivors. This means that you can enjoy a way to grow your savings while at the same time enjoying the peace of mind that comes with knowing that your loved ones are cared for. On top of that, universal life insurance can be used as an estate planning tool to provide liquidity and to protect your estate from the detraction in value that might come as the result of the costs of long-term care.

This type of insurance works in the following way:

- You choose the amount of the death benefit you want. When considering how much coverage to get, consider how much it will take to discharge your various obligations, as well as how much you want for your survivors. If you have dependents (including your spouse or common-law partner), your life insurance death benefit should take into account what amount would be required to provide income—if necessary—after you are gone.
- Your premium is determined, and you make payments to the insurance company. These premium payments are deposited into what is known as a "policy fund." The money is invested by the insurance company in a way that allows it to grow so that the company can pay the benefit on your death.

- Money deposited beyond the cost of insurance can be used to your benefit. You can choose that this extra money be used to make investments that grow tax-deferred over time. This money can be used as you like later on. If you don't feel it necessary to have your money grow on your behalf tax-deferred, you can use the money to increase your death benefit.

You can use your universal life insurance policy in a number of ways that can benefit you now and benefit your estate later.

Estate-planning process.

You can use universal life insurance as part of your estate-planning process. However, it's important that you make sure that universal life insurance is right for your situation and that it will help you accomplish your goals.

In order to determine whether or not universal life insurance is right for you, it's a good idea to go through the estate-planning process. You can do this yourself, or you can get help from a qualified financial professional. Getting help from a professional can be a good idea, since an outside advisor can often help you see your situation in a new light.

The first step is to go on a "fact-finding mission." You need to consider the facts of the situation, and of your retirement. What is your current financial situation? What expectations do you have for the future? What expenses do you expect to have, and how will these obligations affect your overall estate down the road?

Establish the facts of the case and then consider your objectives. If you are working with a financial professional, let him or her know exactly where you stand. You then need to share your objectives. Share what you want your retirement to look like, and your financial planner can help you determine what you need to do in order to reach your goals.

A good financial planner and advisor can analyze your situation and figure out what course of action is most likely to benefit you. In some cases, if you have maxed out your RRSP contributions and other tax-advantaged contributions, a universal life policy can provide you with another route to watch your earnings grow tax-free. If you have a large estate, a universal life policy can be a way to provide your heirs with a simple way to pay taxes and discharge other obligations against your estate.

Depending on your goals and aims, a universal life policy might be just the thing. Once you have determined your course of action, though, you need to implement it. Whether you pay extra for investment purposes, or to increase your death benefit, make a plan and stick with it.

Also, be aware that a universal policy, since it is permanent and doesn't expire at the end of a set term, will be more expensive than term life insurance. Be prepared for this higher cost, and plan accordingly in your implementation of your plan.

Taxation

One of the great advantages of universal life insurance is that the death benefit paid to your survivors is tax-free. This can provide a way for you to provide a tax-free benefit for your survivors, as opposed to the taxes levied against your estate upon your death. If you want more to go to your beneficiaries, a life insurance policy can be a great help.

It's also worth noting that even the amount above the death benefit, as might be accrued through investment, is tax-free. So, your survivors receive the entire amount without the need to pay income tax. This is also true in the case of a split-beneficiary situation. You can designate that one person receives the death benefit and that someone else receives the investment returns. In both cases, though, the recipient doesn't have to pay income tax on the money.

You can also take advantage of the tax-favored status associated with universal life insurance policies. While you will have to pay taxes on dividends received in cash as a result of your universal life policy, you can avoid taxes if you instead direct such dividends to be paid back into the policy. Any dividends paid back into the policy to purchase additional coverage are not taxed, and that can be a benefit to others later.

The tax-exempt growth enjoyed by investments in a universal life policy does have its limits. When you pay extra premiums, and you allocate that money for investments within the policy, you will earn interest. Your money will grow tax-free up to a certain point (as figured by the Canadian Income Tax Act). In order to help you avoid these issues, your coverage can be increased up to 8 percent annually so that more of your premium goes to coverage, rather than having your investment income exceed the limit. However, if you still exceed the limit, realize that you will see the excess taxed as interest income.

Since that can be quite a blow, it is vital that you plan your extra payments to the policy so that you don't end up paying at the interest income rate—which isn't favored in the same way that other investment income is.

Need for estate liquidity

You might be surprised at how much liquidity an estate needs after you pass on. There are costs associated with passing a property on, and these can become onerous to your survivors. First of all, the property you hold at death is subject to estate tax. The federal government wants its share, as does the provincial/territorial government.

On top of that, there might be probate fees. Probate fees are charged by the courts as your property is disposed of according to your wishes. Even if you have a will, probate is still a reality, and the fees will have to be paid for by your estate.

These costs can add up quickly. Your survivors will need the capital to clear these expenses as quickly as possible. However, your assets may be a little illiquid at the time of your death. You might have real estate that is valuable (and taxed accordingly), but the ready cash to pay the tax obligation might not be in existence. Money held in certain accounts, whether they be registered accounts or annuities or some other type of account, might not be easily liquidated.

In the meantime, bills are piling up and your survivors are wondering how they will pay all these obligations. This is where universal life insurance can come in handy. If you have a large-enough policy, your beneficiaries can use the payout to discharge the taxes and the probate fees, as well as other costs that might be incurred. This clears the obligations against the estate. That way, your heirs have more time to liquidate your assets and figure out what to do with them. Life insurance can be a great way to help improve the liquidity of your estate.

You can also use universal life insurance in your charitable-giving efforts. If you wish to bequeath some of your wealth to a good cause, you might consider naming a charity as the beneficiary to your life insurance policy. This provides a more liquid source of funds to the charity than a piece of real property, or the assets in an account.

Plus, naming a charity as your beneficiary can result in a tax deduction for you, even while you live. If a registered charity is the beneficiary of your policy, you will get a donation receipt for your policy amount. You can then use this as a tax deduction. This is a great way for you to be generous, bestow a liquid gift on a good cause, and benefit from a tax deduction. If you are inclined toward philanthropy, this can be a wise course of action—and one that any charity can appreciate.

Universal life benefits during your lifetime

While life insurance is, in the main, designed for you to provide a measure of security and stability to your survivors, you can also benefit during your lifetime. If you have a universal life policy, you can use it to your advantage now; it doesn't have to entirely go to the benefit of your heirs.

First of all, you can use your policy for tax-deferred wealth accumulation. You can pay extra premiums into your policy, and the money will grow tax-deferred, as long as you remain within the limits set by the Canadian Revenue Agency. You can withdraw cash from your policy, and from the accumulated wealth, whenever you want. Check with your policy for minimum withdrawal amounts. Also, realize that your withdrawal might be subject to income tax, and you will likely see a reduction in your coverage. You might also have to pay a partial surrender fee.

You can also cancel your policy, surrendering it entirely, for the accumulated cash value. Once again, there might be surrender fees, and you might have to pay costs associated with the insurance policy that are outstanding. If your universal policy has a guaranteed interest option, there might also be a market-value adjustment. Make sure you understand all of the implications before you take such a step.

It's also possible for you to leverage your universal life policy with a loan. The wealth you have accumulated can be borrowed from at any time, as long as minimum requirements have been met. You might need a specific amount built up for your policy, or you might need to have had your policy for a specified period of time in order to borrow. You can usually choose between variable and fixed-rate loans. Realize that your coverage might be reduced during the loan's terms, and you will have to repay the amount you borrowed with interest.

Your universal life insurance policy can also be used as collateral for other loans. Your cash value continues to grow in this case, and you can access your funds tax-free. When you die, though, the loan (and the interest accumulated) must be repaid through the policy benefit. It's worth noting that when you use your policy as collateral for certain loans, the interest you pay might be tax-deductible.

If you want to improve the tax efficiency of a retirement compensation arrangement (RCA), you can fund it with universal life insurance. With this strategy, you structure your agreement so that you avoid 50 percent of your annual return going to the refundable tax account (RTA) held by the CRA. With the RCA, 50 percent of your employer's contribution and 50 percent of the fund's annual returns go to the RTA. However, if you fund your RCA with a universal life insurance policy, the tax-sheltered funds are not subject to being sent to the RTA—which offers no return.

However, when you set up your RCA this way, a portion of your employer's contribution goes to pay the insurance contract, so you might not see the same retirement benefits later. On top of that, money paid out from the RCA to beneficiaries is taxable—even though the money is held in a life insurance policy. This is because the policy death benefit and the accumulated wealth are distributed (tax-free) to the RCA. Only then is it passed on to the beneficiaries.

If you want to reduce the problems associated with this situation, you can consult a knowledgeable financial planner about strategies such as shared ownership that can reduce the tax impact after your death.

Another benefit of universal life insurance comes in the form of creditor protection. Your life insurance policy is protected from the demands of creditors in certain circumstances. In some cases, your life insurance policy might not even be considered part of your estate and be exempted from creditor demands. As long as you don't surrender your life insurance policy during your lifetime for its cash value, you can use life insurance, with a properly set up contract, as protection from creditors. Consult with a knowledgeable professional for more information about how this can be done and the protections you may be entitled to.

Don't let long-term care and other issues diminish your retirement funds. Back your assets with proper insurance.

CHAPTER SEVEN:

RETIREMENT WEALTH THROUGH STOCKS

Build wealth with your stock portfolio

One of the realities of wealth building is that, while it's nice to think that cash products and "safe" investments like GICs can provide you with a guaranteed return, few asset classes can provide you with the return necessary to build a nest egg able to see you through retirement.

Cash might be safe, and you might have the benefit of a guaranteed return with GICs, but the yield on these safe assets is usually so small that wealth building over time isn't practical. Indeed, in some cases, you would be hard-pressed to see any real gain after inflation does its job on your purchasing power. Consider: if inflation is relatively conservative, at 2.5

percent per year, but your cash investments only earn you 2 percent each year, you are actually losing 0.5 percent each year in real terms.

Even if inflation weren't an issue, the yield on a "safer" asset really isn't enough to help you build sufficient wealth over time. When you consider that your cash or GIC investment yields such a small return, you'll realize that your guaranteed investment is unlikely to help you earn anything substantial in the long run. If you set aside $500 a month for thirty years, and you earn 2 percent a year, compounded monthly, your future value will be $236,362.69. That's not even close to enough to retire on—and that doesn't even account for inflation and taxes.

There are a number of online calculators that can help you run the numbers, doing the math to illustrate the realities of compound interest. Now, what if you set aside that same $500 a month for thirty years, but instead of getting a 2 percent return in cash, you managed an annualized return of 8 percent because you invested in stocks? Your total would be $745,179.72. That's a little more like it.

Compounding returns

Compound returns are the key to a successful retirement portfolio. You need to invest in a way that your money earns money. Compounding returns is basically the idea that your growth earns more growth. So, when you invest capital and see a return above what you originally invested, that gain, in turn, is invested and provides you with even more money down the road. Compounding returns are about making sure that your earnings continue to earn even more money. It's better than simple interest, in which you just receive the interest earnings from your capital, and nothing more happens with those returns.

Compounding returns are most effective when you have the chance at a higher annualized yield. The reality is that building your entire portfolio around low-yielding assets is a long road to frustration with your portfolio's growth. If you want to be ready for your retirement future, you need to be willing to invest in stocks. Yes, you should keep a portion of your portfolio in "safer" assets like cash and bonds. However, you don't want to rely too heavily on these investments. Instead, they should form a portion of your portfolio designed as a backstop against market volatility that will always be present.

While you're building a portfolio, it makes sense to consider your asset allocation and consider that it doesn't make sense to eschew stocks, especially during the building phase of your retirement portfolio. You can build a nest egg more efficiently with stocks, since the potential annualized return is much higher than with cash or GICs.

When you invest in GICs, your return is locked in for a set period of years. Market conditions won't change that. With cash, changes can come, but those changes are small, and you will be lucky if your cash returns outpace inflation. Stocks, on the other hand, range from losses to large gains. Consistently investing in stocks provides you with the opportunity to take advantage of bigger returns. Even considering years when the stock market loses, over time the bigger gains in certain years more than offset the losses. It's not unusual to see stocks offer annualized returns of 7 to 10 percent when averaged over periods of decades. That just doesn't happen with GICs or cash.

However, that doesn't mean that you should just dive in and start stock picking. That can easily lead to disaster. Instead, it's a good idea to consider establishing a relationship with a portfolio manager.

Hire a Portfolio Manager

Managed portfolios provide you with a good way to take advantage of the wealth-growing potential of stocks without some of the risks of picking "wrong" individual stocks for your portfolio.

Stock picking vs. a professionally managed portfolio

When unsophisticated investors think about investing in stocks, they immediately think about stock picking. With stock picking, you buy shares of one stock at a time, composing your portfolio of individual stocks chosen by you. The problem with unsophisticated stock picking is that it is so easy to choose the "wrong" stock, with little thought going towards the necessary portfolio principles such as asset allocation, diversification and sector rotation

Individual stocks are subject to the whims of the market, as well as to other factors. An individual stock could suffer a crippling blow when its CEO is discovered as corrupt. The target market could reject the products and services offered by the company. Mismanagement could sink the stock. Changing attitudes could render the company irrelevant.

With amateur stock picking, you are pinning your hopes for future retirement wealth on the performances of single stocks with no cohesive portfolio plan. An experienced qualified portfolio manager will ensure you establish a disciplined approach to your investment portfolio.

Let's say you have $500 to set aside each month in your retirement savings efforts. You want to make sure you have a diverse portfolio, so you decide to put $100 of it in GICs and put the other $400 in four different stocks, chosen for their diversity across industry and sector. You put $100 a month in each of these four stocks:

1. Stock A's price is $40 a share, allowing you to buy 2.5 shares.
2. Stock B's price is $100 a share, allowing you to buy one share.
3. Stock C's price is $150 a share, allowing you to buy 2/3 of a share.
4. Stock D's price is $80 a share, allowing you to buy 1.25 shares.

You aren't going to be able to purchase very many shares overall each month if you look only at getting high-quality (and more expensive) shares that you can reasonably expect to stand the test of time. If the stock price goes up, you'll be able to purchase even fewer. Plus, your portfolio is set up to be somewhat risky. What if one of those stocks completely tanks? That's a pretty significant portion of your portfolio, and it runs the risk of bringing your entire retirement hopes down.

Individual stock picking sets you up for a great chance of failure over time. Sure, there is a chance that you might get lucky and hit on just the right stock purchase at the right time. But it's far more likely that your individual stock choices will be buffeted about by stock market volatility.

A managed portfolio, on the other hand, provides you with a certain amount of protection. With a managed portfolio, your entire investment goes toward a group of stocks chosen for their specific characteristics. If one of the investments in the portfolio underperforms, it is removed from the mix—without impacting your portfolio returns significantly.

Instead of basing your returns on the hope that a few individual stocks will appreciate appropriately over time, you benefit from the overall performance of a group of specifically chosen stocks. It's possible to invest in a managed portfolio that is diverse enough to fulfill your needs. A professionally managed portfolio can provide investors with the proper asset allocation and diversification necessary to generate positive long-term returns well above the rate of inflation. These accounts are usually less expensive than mutual funds and allow a portfolio manager to tailor the account specifically to the exact needs of each individual.

Managed portfolios vs. index funds

Many investors like to use index funds, since they make it easy for you to invest, and because they come with low costs. Also, there has been a big deal made of the fact that managed funds can underperform the market. Index funds are easier for the do-it-yourselfer to invest in because they just track an index. Many do-it-yourselfers stick with all-market index funds, which simply track the combined performance of everything in a particular market.

While this sounds like an easy way to invest in stocks, the reality is that, even with the low costs associated with index funds, you will never be able to beat the market. If you are investing with the market, using an index fund, you will always come out behind after fees and taxes are figured in.

A managed portfolio, has the potential to beat the market. The key, though, is finding the right manager for you. The right managed portfolio, has the possibility of superseding market performance. It gives you a chance to come out ahead, even after you consider taxes and fees.

But you have to be careful. Picking a portfolio manager is serious business. A recent survey found that 74 percent of actively managed mutual funds underperformed in the last three years. With your own quality portfolio manager your potential for outperformance is much better.

Why do many active mutual fund managers fail? One of the biggest reasons is frequent trading (and its attendant costs), and a penchant to try and chase the next "big thing." Even the most experienced of mutual fund managers make mistakes, and it's important to be aware of that. Quite often there are cost advantages in managed portfolios versus mutual funds and investors should be aware of this.

It makes sense to look for a good money manager. This isn't about choosing actively managed mutual funds; it's about finding someone who can help you manage all aspects of your retirement portfolio to get the best results from your money.

The dangers of do-it-yourself retirement investing

There are very real dangers associated with do-it-yourself retirement investing. First of all, you might not have the understanding or expertise to create a long-term investing plan. While just about anyone can learn the basics of investing and asset allocation and how to create a long-term strategy for a successful retirement, it takes time and effort. While it's important for everyone to have a grasp of what's happening with their portfolios, it's not necessary to be an expert.

In fact, you probably have a day job, and a family. When you aren't at your job, wouldn't you rather be relaxing or spending time with your loved ones instead of trying to manage your assets? While you do want an idea of the overall plan, and how it all works, and you should be able to understand the investments in your portfolio, you might not want to go through the rigorous training and education it takes to become an expert.

A good portfolio manager can help in this area. He or she understands the ins and outs and the best practices. Rather than you spending all that time to become an expert, you can hire someone who already is. One of the best uses of your resources is hiring people who are more efficient than you in certain areas.

Another issue that many do-it-yourselfers run into is an overabundance of emotion. When there is market volatility, it's hard to stand back and stick to your retirement plan. Panic sets in, and it's easy these days to just sign in to your online brokerage account and make a move that you'll end up regretting later. It's almost always a bad idea to make financial decisions when you're under the influence of strong emotion, whether that emotion is excitement or fear. A good money manager can look at things calmly and help keep you on track, explaining why the long-term strategy is likely to provide you with success over time.

Too often, do-it-yourselfers simply lose track of the long-term goals and realities of the situation when faced with short-term volatility. A good money manager can help you take your mind off the current troubles and help you focus on the long-term end result.

How to choose a good money manager

You want to find a skilled money manager who can help you create the right long-term retirement strategy for you. Here are some things to look for as you choose a money manager:

- **Certifications**: The first thing to look for is some sort of certification. You want a reputable money manager who has had official training. Check his or her credentials, and verify them. It's possible to verify credentials by checking an association website or checking with provincial records. Before you turn your money over, make sure the manager's certifications are legitimate and up-to-date.
- **Reviews**: Find out if the money manager will provide you with references. Talk to those who have used the services or check online review sites. You can also look for ethics violations and reprimands. If your potential money manager is clean, then you can have more trust for him or her.
- **Transparent fees**: You will have to pay fees no matter what, to access a money manager. Look for someone who is transparent and open about the fees and how they are charged. Watch out for managers who receive most of their pay from commissions paid for recommending certain products. In these cases, it can be tempting for a manager to invest your money in a fund that offers a higher

commission instead of in an investment product that is in your best interest. There are plenty of money managers with transparent fees, who only charge you a percentage of your assets under management. In these cases, the manager has an interest in you doing well, since the better your portfolio does, the more money he or she makes.

- **Someone who doesn't make outrageous claims**: Even the most skilled money managers aren't always going to come out ahead. Everyone has bad years—especially during market downturns. Your portfolio will lose value at some point. Anyone who tells you that he or she has a "system" that prevents loss even during the worst of down cycles probably isn't to be trusted. Instead, talk to your money manager about the realities of the situation and the possibilities of economic problems impacting your portfolio. The best money managers are those that craft a long-term strategy that ensures that your portfolio recovers fairly smoothly after a market event.

- **A method for keeping you informed**: A good money manager keeps you informed about your portfolio and talks to you about the possible options. He or she should be able to explain, in understandable language, all of the investments that he or she chooses for your retirement portfolio. He or she should also encourage you to be an educated investor. Yes, you are entrusting someone else with your portfolio. But that doesn't mean that you should be ignorant of what's going on. A good money manager keeps you informed and updated on your portfolio and explains your options.

Most money managers are willing to talk to you for a half hour or an hour, free of charge, so that you can see if you are a good fit. If someone doesn't sit well with you, move on. Choose someone with a long-term outlook that you know is going to be ethical and disciplined.

Ask about his or her investment approach to get a feel for whether or not this is someone you can trust with your portfolio over time. You also want to make sure that your potential money manager adheres to the basic, time-tested principles of growing wealth over time.

Asset allocation and diversification

One of the items to consider as you choose a money manager is to consider his or her asset allocation style. Specifically, your money manager should help you create an asset allocation method that works well for you. Historically, asset allocation has mattered more than the particular investments that are actually chosen. Asset allocation allows you to take advantage of the growth expected in a particular asset class. An asset class—stocks, bonds, cash, currencies, commodities, etc.—comes with shared traits related to risk. Generally, stocks are considered riskier than bonds or cash, but less risky than currencies and commodities.

Stocks make an excellent middle ground when it comes to investing because they are easy to trade and easy to understand. Additionally, over time, stocks tend to do well. In a twenty-five-year period, stocks have yet to come out behind. The way you choose to divide up the assets in your retirement portfolio can make a big difference over time.

Not too long ago, Vanguard put together a historical look at different allocations of stocks and bonds and historical performance from 1926 to 2012. This can give you a good idea of what you can expect, long-term, from different asset allocations.

A 100 percent bond investment from 1926 to 2012 would have resulted in a 5.5 percent average annual return, with only thirteen out of the eighty-seven years resulting in losses. This approach allows investors to feel that their money is safe. It also provides stable income. However, you aren't going to build wealth very quickly. On the other hand, an investment of 100 percent stocks would have resulted in an average annual return of 10 percent over the same period. But there were twenty-five years of loss sprinkled throughout. You need a strong stomach to deal with the kind of uncertainty that comes with relying on such a volatile portfolio—especially since there is the possibility of a market downturn just before you retire.

The timing of a market downturn matters. This is where prudent asset allocation comes in. During the early years of your portfolio, known as the "building" phase, it's better to have a higher percentage of stocks in your portfolio. An allocation of 80 percent stocks and 20 percent bonds between 1926 and 2012 would have resulted in an average annual return of 9.4 percent. That's not bad at all, and it includes an income component.

If you start out with an aggressive portfolio, your money manager can help you shift your assets as your retirement approaches. At the beginning of your building phase, an aggressive portfolio, weighted toward stocks, makes sense. You can see your nest egg grow as quickly as it needs to. However, as retirement gets closer, your money manager can help you conservatise your portfolio. By switching to a more conservative portfolio at retirement, you still preserve an ability to grow your portfolio, but most of it is well protected and providing you income—right when you need the income to support you during retirement.

A changing asset allocation is important because a sharp drop in the stock market just prior to your retirement, or in the first few years of your retirement, can mean that you aren't able to maintain your lifestyle. If you adjust so that you have more assets in income investments that are relatively safe, you won't have to worry as much about the stock market drop because the principal used to invest in your income assets will be mostly preserved.

Diversification

An important part of this equation is diversification. Diversification is first about asset class. This is why many portfolios are divided between stocks, bonds, and cash reserves. This diversification provides a measure of protection so that all is not lost if one asset class goes through a rough patch. Some money managers might even help you diversify your holdings further with the help of real estate (REITs pay dividends and can add another asset class to your portfolio without the need for large capital outlay) or ETFs based on commodities or currencies.

It's important, though, to focus mainly on asset classes that fit your risk profile and that are likely to provide you with the mix of growth and income that you need at each stage of your life.

Diversification is more than an asset class though. It also includes sectors and industries. If all of your stock holdings are in a single industry, and that industry fails, you are in trouble. You need to make sure that you are diversified in different areas within asset classes. A good money manager can help you figure out what is appropriate for your long-term goals.

It's also important to include geographic diversity in your portfolio. Domestic investments are great, but you should also consider foreign investments. Adding well-chosen foreign stocks and bonds to your portfolio can provide you with the ability to take advantage of growth elsewhere. In many cases, there are foreign markets that offer growth when things stagnate at home. Getting help adding some of those to your portfolio can help with your portfolio-building efforts. There are plenty of investment assets from various countries. Get outside our borders, and you might be surprised at what you can accomplish.

Dividend-paying stocks in your retirement portfolio

One of the best ways to build wealth and cultivate income in your retirement portfolio is with the help of dividend-paying stocks. Some companies pay out some of their profits to shareholders, providing them with income on top of capital appreciation.

Adding dividend-paying stocks to your retirement portfolio can benefit you during the building stage of your portfolio and during the income phase. There are some companies that, even during times of economic turmoil and stock market downturn, still make payouts. These companies, known as "dividend aristocrats," are generally solid choices that have stood the test of time. There are also managed portfolios composed of dividend-paying stocks. These portfolios offer you access to a variety of dividend-paying investments, limiting your exposure to risk and providing you with the opportunity to gain income and enhance capital appreciation.

During the growth stage of your portfolio, it may make sense to invest in assets with dividend reinvestment. A dividend reinvestment plan is one in which the dividends paid out to you are automatically reinvested. If you have one hundred shares of a dividend stock that pays out fifty cents per share every quarter, this means that you get fifty dollars every three months. If your dividends are reinvested, you basically end up with "free" shares. If the stock costs fifty dollars per share, then you add one additional share to your portfolio every quarter. At the end of the year, you now have 104 shares, and your payout increases to fifty-two dollars each quarter. And, of course, those extra shares also have the potential for capital appreciation on top of the increased dividend earnings.

This is just a simple illustration, and the amounts seem small, but consider if you followed this pattern over the course of thirty years while you build your retirement portfolio. The dividends, combined with compound returns, would be formidable. Put such a solution in the hands of an experienced money manager who understands asset allocation and how to make the most of your money with the help of dividend funds and proper diversification, and you are likely to experience a remarkably successful retirement, no matter the day-to-day volatility seen in the current climate.

CHAPTER EIGHT:

WHAT HISTORY TELLS US

History is on the side of stocks

While past performance doesn't guarantee future results, the reality is that history can give us an idea of what to expect. Something that does well consistently over time is likely to continue to do well in the future. There might be hiccups along the way, but an asset that has done well for decades is likely to continue doing well. Stocks fall into that category.

Over time, even though market volatility can lead to steep losses in a single year, or even a group of five years, stocks tend to do well over long periods. If you look at stock market performance trend lines, they look pretty choppy over a short period of time. Stock market volatility is quite pronounced when you look at price swings over a period of a year—or even two or three.

When you look at stock performance over longer periods, though, the trend line smooth's out.

Stock returns since the 1900s

One of the realities of the stock market is that, on a day-to-day basis, it looks as though things are quite volatile. Even if you look at stock market performance over the course of a decade, the situation appears quite volatile. However, when you take a step back and look at the entire picture, long term market performance looks quite attractive.

While the Dow Jones Industrial Average in the United States is only a sampling of stocks, it nevertheless provides us with a good illustration of the trend in stocks.

As you can see, since 1900, stock prices have been on a steady climb. This chart doesn't get into the second decade of the 2000s, but it does illustrate the point well. The trend line is rather pronounced. If you keep your money in over decades, say investing from now until you retire, there is a good chance that you will experience excellent growth. If you can resist the urge to panic and sell at a low point.

Dow Jones Industrial Average 1900- present

It's also interesting to note that, even during troughs, you can still come out ahead—depending on when you put your money in. Consider, if you had bought shares in 1900, even the big crash that kicked off the Great Depression wouldn't have seen you in that bad of shape. Over the course of the thirty-year period between 1900 and 1930, stocks lose little value. Yes, it was a shock from the levels reached a couple of years earlier, but for the long-term investor, with an eye to the big picture, things would have turned out.

And that's how you need to view your retirement—as part of a long-term plan. Retirement investing isn't about the short term; it's about the long trend.

Why have stock prices gained dramatically since the 1900s?

Looking at the above chart, it's obvious that stock prices have been gaining rather dramatically since the 1900s. Some of that has to do with the expansion of the stock market and the accessibility of the stock market. Back in the 1900s, very few people could afford to invest. Indeed, you probably notice a rather pronounced increase in stock prices from 1950 onward.

The availability of money since the United States and other countries moved away from currencies backed by precious metals (gold and/or silver), the changes in the global economy, the spread of technology and the service economy in the first world, and other factors are contributing to an unprecedented amount of wealth that nearly anyone can access.

Consider: even thirty years ago, you needed to have a significant amount of capital and access to a stockbroker to execute trades on the stock market. Now, all you need is a computer with internet access and twenty-five dollars in your online brokerage account. On top of that, the rise of tax-advantaged retirement accounts, such as RRSPs here in Canada and 401(k)s in the United States, has also contributed to the increase in participation in the stock market.

With more participation, there has been an increase in prices. With economic expansion, there is more money going around, and without limiting the supply of money by tying it to a specific standard, there is more of it available to everyone. Whether you agree with the idea of a fiat currency or not, the reality of today's global economy is that availability and accessibility have done their work, and stock prices continue to rise.

Long-term bond returns

The common alternative to stocks is bonds. Bonds are considered safe—especially if they are backed by a government. Bonds basically represent loans. When you invest in a bond, you are loaning money to a company or a government or some other entity. Because the organization pays you back over time (with interest), the feeling is that a bond is safer than a stock.

When you invest in a stock, you take your chance that it will improve in value and that someone later on will buy it from you for more than you paid. With a bond, you are promised that, after a set period of time, the entity will return your principal. Plus, in the meantime, you receive regular interest payments.

However, the perceived security of a bond means that you don't see the same level of returns as you see with stocks. It's true that you can lose your principal (and any interest not yet paid) if the government or company defaults on its obligations. This is why a company or government that is considered stable offers lower yields. If you are willing to take a bigger risk, and invest in an entity that is considered likely to default, you have the chance at a higher return.

Many bond investors, though, are more interested in a relatively stable source of income. And that's a good thing, since, over time, the "safest" of bonds are unlikely to provide adequate returns for building wealth. Ibbotson Associates reports that, since 1926, US government bonds have returned, on average, between 5 percent and 6 percent per year. That should be compared to the average annual return of 9.8 percent seen by stocks.

Corporate bonds fare a little bit better than government bonds, but not by much. This trend is present in Canada as well. According to the *GFD Guide to Total Returns on Stocks, Bonds, and Bills*, there have been decades in which bonds outperformed equities. However, even considering these periods of time, in general equities offer better returns than bonds over time.

Using a handy calculator from The Globe and Mail, it's possible to see that between 1936 and 2011, the annualized returns for bonds in Canada was 6.96 percent (as compared to stocks at 9.53 percent). If you were to invest $500 a month for thirty years for your retirement, you would see a huge difference in what you end up with over time: $601,866.24 for bonds versus $989,280.67 for stocks. Basically, the difference between retiring a millionaire and not reaching that goal depends on your asset allocation.

Over the long haul, bonds just aren't going to offer the same returns.

Long-term gold and commodity prices

Many investors attempt to inject a little growth in their portfolios by adding gold and other commodities. These assets are also often included in portfolios because they are seen as hedges against inflation. Often, gold prices move inversely to the US dollar, gaining when the dollar falls in value.

Because commodities are denominated in US dollars, they are seen as useful additions to portfolios when the fear is that inflation is taking over as the purchasing power of the greenback drops. It also helps matters that the Canadian dollar is considered a commodity currency (due especially to its relationship with oil).

However, even so, relying too heavily on commodities can be an issue. It's true that gold prices have skyrocketed in recent years. For nearly two hundred years, from 1717 to 1914, the price of gold was fairly steady, set by Isaac Newton and denominated in the British currency. However, many factors have influenced the changes in gold prices. Gold is influenced more by perception and market forces now, and currencies are no longer tied to commodities for value.

The average price of gold in 2007 was $695.39, and it has jumped dramatically since then, to $1,243 an ounce at the time of this writing. At one point, though, gold almost reached $2,000 an ounce. Gold rose rapidly as stimulus efforts by the US government led to inflation fears, and a worry that the US dollar was on the verge of collapse. Since then, however, those fears are easing, and gold prices have decoupled somewhat from the US dollar. It's been an interesting phenomenon to watch.

One of the issues that comes with investing in gold and other precious metals is that you can end up paying a premium, especially if you invest in physical commodities. The premium paid, not to mention costs associated with storing the metals and other concerns, can eat into real returns.

Other commodities, such as oil, are equally volatile. Oil prices see huge price spikes over time, followed by huge drops. Like gold, oil traditionally moves inversely to the US dollar. One of the issues with oil is that it is very influenced by geopolitical situations, as well as being sensitive to anything that might indicate supply difficulties, such as problems with oil rigs and refineries.

Stock returns

Many of the returns presented thus far are based on nominal returns. It's important to realize that there is a difference in the way returns are reported. Nominal returns are just the numbers; they don't take into account such factors as inflation.

Inflation erodes your actual returns. In the case of the returns offered by stocks and bonds in Canada from 1936 to 2011, the nominal returns were 9.53 percent and 6.96 percent, respectively. However, the story changes once growth is adjusted for inflation. Inflation, which is represented in the increase in price or reduction in buying power, is the reason that your money doesn't go as far as it used to. As the money supply has increased over time, and as the global economy has picked up the pace and added volume, prices have risen with the ability of consumers to pay them.

One dollar twenty years from now will be unable to buy the same amount as measured in goods and services as a dollar today. All you have to do is think back to your childhood. How much did a candy bar cost when you were growing up? And how much does it cost now? Chances are that you get less candy for your buck now than you did when you were a child.

In the case of Canadian stocks and bonds, once you add inflation into equation, returns between 1936 and 2011 suddenly become 5.58 percent for stocks and 3.10 percent for bonds. Add in somewhat modest MERs, and *The Globe and Mail* figures that stocks earned 4.02 percent and bonds earned 2.18 percent in this scenario. That's a real wake-up call.

Your real returns are going to be based on what happens when inflation, taxes, and fees take their cut of your investments. The reality is that if you want to be able to come out ahead over time, you need to take advantage of good risk in a way that allows for reasonable growth without taking on too much risk.

With stocks, we must consider dividends as well as capital appreciation. Capital appreciation is what you end up with in terms of the difference between what you pay for an asset and what you end up selling it for. Dividends, though, can augment your real returns. A dividend payment is money you receive just for being a shareholder. This is one of the ways you can boost your real returns. Dividend income comes with favorable tax treatment, so that helps in terms of preserving some of your purchasing power over time. Adding dividends into the equation can boost your real returns over time.

In fact, once you include dividends in the equation, the average return over any ten year period since 1937 has been 127 percent. That's pretty good. Adding dividends into the equation can make a difference. Adding dividend-paying stocks to your retirement portfolio can help you overcome some of the difficulties presented when you start thinking about real returns.

Even with real returns taken into account, though, stocks outperform many other asset classes.

Fixed-income assets' real returns

Fixed-income assets, such as GICs, are popular because they represent the opportunity for you to see stable revenue each month. However, it's important to note that the returns offered aren't that spectacular. Between 1969 and 2009, GICs returned 2.35 percent above inflation. When taxes are included in the mix, the returns are even worse, depending on your tax bracket.

As you might imagine, while GICs are sometimes attractive to some retirees and can be part of a good retirement portfolio, the reality is that fixed-income assets aren't going to be a great help in actually building your nest egg.

WHAT HISTORY TELLS US

Returns after a stock market crash

The hardest thing about long-term investing is maintaining your cool during a stock market crash. The latest crash is a great example—especially if you look at the United States. When the Dow dropped in 2008 and 2009, many people panicked and pulled their money out of their accounts. Unfortunately, this action merely served to lock in losses. As of this writing, the Dow Jones Industrial Average is in the neighborhood of 16,000. That's quite the recovery from lows of recent memory, which saw the Dow almost down to 6,500.

It's also important to note that, while some individual stocks might not recover so well from a crash, the market as a whole often recovers. Indeed, solid surges are often seen in the years following a big drop. Holding a high quality balanced portfolio of individual stocks, will serve you well if the stocks are solid dividend producers as well. (Dividend aristocrats can be good choices), you might find that you do quite well indeed following a market crash.

History is quite clear: over time, stocks win out over just about every asset class. Average annual returns are better, and even if there is some volatility, stock performance tends to smooth out over time, showing a trend line that point's higher.

CHAPTER NINE:

STOCK AVERAGES AND RETURNS

Choosing your stocks carefully

While stock returns, as a whole, have been impressive, it's important to take into account various factors when deciding what to add to your investment portfolio. As you create a strategy for growing your wealth for retirement, and for maintaining it during retirement, make sure you understand how to best take advantage of the superior returns offered by stocks.

Are stock prices driven by earnings or dividends?

One of the things to be aware of as you consider your retirement portfolio is the way stock prices are determined. In many cases, they are determined by market forces. When market participants feel as though things are going well for a company, they are likely to be willing to pay more to purchase shares, since they think that the price will rise in the future. There is demand for the stock, and prices go up. On the other hand, if it appears that a company might be in trouble, current shareholders want to get rid of their equity and will sell. As more people become interested in selling than in buying, the price drops as sellers accept less in the hopes that they can just get rid of the investment before it falls even further.

To a certain extent, all stocks go through the ups and downs associated with buying and selling. There is always waxing and waning interest in any investment.

But what causes investors to decide whether or not they think a stock will gain or lose value? Some of what influences prices has to do with the reports companies file regularly.

Earnings

One of the biggest factors in determining a stock's value is the earnings report. Companies report their earnings each quarter, and investors are always interested to see how the numbers stand. A good earnings report, with an increase in the amount earned, can mean an increase in stock prices. Higher earnings are usually a sign that a company is doing well.

Earnings can also be reported in terms of how they are related to other important measures. Earnings might be good, but what about the costs? Earnings aren't the same as profits. If there are high costs, or if there are losses in other areas, the earnings are eaten up. You also have to consider liabilities, total assets, profit margins, and other information if you are going to make a decision about which stocks to pick and which not to pick.

Stock prices might also be impacted by dividend yields. However, the impact is rather indirect. An increase in the dividend yield can indicate strength in a company, in turn providing confidence and expectations for future growth. Additionally, higher dividend yields can also make a stock more attractive, since it provides the chance for increased returns for investors. It's important to be careful though; high yields are rarely sustainable over a long period of time. On top of that, some companies boost their dividends in an effort to attract investors—even though they might not be that strong. It's important to think twice before deciding that a specific stock is strong based on its yield, alone.

Composition of stock indexes

Stock indexes are composed by following the performances of a collection of stocks. It's important to note that a stock index is not something you can invest in directly. It's more of a construct designed to give you an idea of how a group of stocks, together, is performing. The prices of selected stocks are used to determine the overall "value" of a segment of the stock market.

Indexes are usually classified by what they track. Global stock indexes usually track a collection of stocks from around the world, usually focusing on prominent companies. National indexes do the same, but with stocks from particular countries. The TSX tracks top Canadian stocks, the FTSE 100 tracks top UK stocks, and the DIJA tracks top US stocks.

It's also possible for indexes to subdivide into smaller sections of the market. There are indexes that track sector or industry stocks, like biotechnology, services, resources, and even real estate. You can find indexes that track groups of stocks with similar market capitalizations.

Other indexes track high-yield dividend stocks. No matter your goals, there are probably indexes that can help you reach them.

Also realize that some indexes are weighted. This means that certain stocks have a greater influence over the performance of the index than other stocks. So the performance of the index might be affected by the fact that a stock with a heavier weighting (perhaps due to its market capitalization) is performing especially well or especially poorly. Keep this fact in mind, and make sure you understand how an index is weighted before you begin investing.

How do you invest in an index if you can't buy shares directly?

Because of the way indexes are composed, you can't directly buy shares in a specific index. That isn't that big of a deal, though, because you can still gain exposure to the stocks on the index with the help of securities like index funds and ETFs.

Index funds are funds constructed in a way that mimics the stocks contained on an index. These are low-cost because they require a minimum of management, since all it takes is buying or selling shares in the individual stocks in the fund based on the index. A similar process is followed when putting together index ETFs. One of the advantages of index ETFs is that it is easier to trade them than it is to trade shares of index mutual funds. You can trade an ETF as if it's a single stock, and do it in real time (the index mutual fund is traded, as with all funds, at the end of the day).

If you want to invest in a particular index, the chances are that your broker—or your employer's RRSP offerings—has an index mutual fund or ETF that tracks the index you are interested in.

It's also worth noting that there are indexes that track bonds as well, so if you are interested in asset class diversification or a little income, it's possible to invest in index funds and ETFs that follow different bond indexes (which can also be classified by country and by sector).

TSX index

The Canada Stock Market (known as S&P/TSX or TSX) has been tracked since 1919. As with many stock markets, the TSX has seen solid growth over time. The chart below illustrates the performance of the TSX since 1975:

Dow Jones Industrial Average Index

The changes in the Canadian stock market haven't been as dramatic as seen in some other world markets, but there is still a definite upward trend line. Indeed, it is much to Canada's credit that its market has seen less volatility than many other markets.

According to Morningstar, the five-year return for the S&P/TSX Composite is 10.57 percent. That's not too bad, but it does mean that the index has been taking advantage of the recovery from the stock market drop following the global financial crisis. Over the last ten years, the TSX has seen a return of 75 percent.

There are index funds and ETFs that follow the TSX and that are inexpensive. You can enjoy the solid returns offered by the TSX for a low cost. Don't forget, too, that you can boost your real returns with the help of dividends, since many of those stocks also offer regular payouts.

S&P index

Don't confine yourself to Canada, however. The S&P 500 index in the United States also offers a good opportunity to invest in a very wide swath of the market. The United States accounts for a very large portion of the world's stock market.

One of the great things about the S&P 500 is the fact that it allows you greater access to the broader US stock market. There is a lot of emphasis placed on the Dow Jones Industrial Average, but the reality is that the DIJA looks at only thirty stocks. Investing in an index based on the DIJA doesn't give you the same breadth. When you are looking to reduce your risk while investing in stocks, breadth is important.

The annualized return for the S&P 500 (including its precursor, the S&P 90) was in the neighborhood of 9.77 percent between 1926 and 2011. Even during one of the worst five-year periods for the S&P 500 (the period ending with 2011), the return was only − 0.25 percent. Remember that this period encompassed a rather difficult time period.

One of the great things about the S&P 500 is the fact that there are solid returns over time. While real returns are going to be eroded by inflation and taxes, the fact remains that the S&P 500 still is one of the indexes to watch over time. Like so many other stock indexes, it is possible to invest in ETFs and index funds that track the S&P 500. You don't have to worry as much about the performances of individual stocks when your returns are based instead on the movements of the wider market. This means that, over time, your portfolio is likely to increase in value.

How diversification increases returns while reducing risk

One of the reasons to get involved in index investing is due to the diversification. With index investing, you get exposure to several securities at once, rather than relying on your stock-picking skills to tide you over.

Diversification allows you to get access to more securities, so that if the individual performance of a stock is poor, it doesn't necessarily mean the performance of your entire portfolio will be poor. One of the components of an index might drop, but if all of the rest of the equities on the index are doing well, your overall performance is positive. This is much harder to accomplish in a portfolio with a small number of securities.

You also have the ability to diversify on a number of other levels with the help of index investing. For instance, if you want to diversify across geography (and you should), you can invest in countries that might do well even when Canada is faltering. You might invest in a world index to help offset the times when the TSX is doing poorly. You can also invest in different sectors. If biotech is struggling, resources might be doing well. Having a little of each can help you reduce volatility through diversification.

Diversification also works across asset classes. There are indexes that follow commodities, currencies, real estate, stocks, and bonds. While you might not want to diversify too much, it can be helpful to build the bulk of your portfolio out of stocks and bond indexes, and then add a little real estate and commodities to the mix. Make sure you consult with a knowledgeable financial planner to help you figure out what mix of assets is most appropriate for your retirement goals and your risk tolerance.

Foreign stocks and currency risk

One thing you have to watch out for as you diversify is the currency risk that comes with purchasing foreign stocks. When you buy on a foreign stock exchange, you might have to have your own currency converted to the currency used by that specific market. Since currency rates fluctuate frequently, this could mean that you run the risk of losing—even when you think you're winning—because of the way your currency stands with regard to the foreign currency.

If you are concerned about this issue, speak with a knowledgeable financial adviser about how you can diversify using your own currency. In many cases, it's possible to gain exposure to foreign assets with the help of index funds and ETFs. You can diversify geographically without taking on the foreign exchange risk.

Risks of investing in small caps

The default mode of investing in stocks is often to choose stocks with large market capitalization. In order to add diversity, some investors like to add small-cap stocks to their portfolios. This can be one way to add growth. Often, small-cap stocks have potential for significant growth. Investing in a small-cap index can boost your retirement portfolio's returns.

Unfortunately, there are also risks with small-cap stocks. In many cases, these are stocks that haven't achieved the long-term success seen by large-cap stocks. As a result, you might be taking a bigger risk. Additionally, returns can be volatile, and if dividends are involved, you are unlikely to see measurable, sustainable growth. At the first sign of trouble, a small-cap stock is likely to cut its payout.

Take these risks into consideration before you devote too many resources to small-cap stocks and small-cap index funds. During retirement, it makes more sense to look into solid assets that provide a little more stability and long-term predictability.

Value stocks vs. growth stocks

Rather than getting caught up in small caps and large caps, consider the question of growth versus value. Both types of stocks have a place in your portfolio, but you need to consider your long-term retirement goals and needs over time.

Growth stocks

Growth stocks are those invested in primarily for their potential gains. Normally, these stocks are those that are likely to see dramatic capital appreciation over time—and perhaps be accompanied by high-dividend yields.

As always, though, the risk of higher potential returns comes with the risk of higher potential losses. When you are younger, you might have time to recover from a mistake made with growth stocks. During retirement, though, dramatic growth isn't the goal, especially since a mistake can mean serious problems with the long-term sustainability of your retirement portfolio.

Value stocks

These are stocks that have a little more steady and solid growth over time. These aren't stocks that are likely to see dramatic gains, but they are likely to have long-term staying power. You are likely to see modest capital appreciation over time. If dividends are involved, the yields are likely to be in the 2 percent to 5 percent range.

Value stocks are just what they sound like—a good value for your money. You pay a reasonable amount for these stocks, and you can expect reasonable and steady appreciation over time. Inclusion of value assets in your retirement portfolio can result in modest growth, enough to help sustain your portfolio and income over time, but not put it at risk.

This is where indexing can help as well. Investing in index assets (mutual funds and ETFs) that focus on value assets can provide you with a lower-risk way to invest in stocks. You get the benefit of modest growth that can ensure you don't outlive your money, but without the risks that come with stock picking. On top of that, you avoid some of the volatility that can come with growth assets. During retirement, value index investments can be a way to maintain your peace of mind.

Deferring taxes on your investments

We've talked a little bit about strategies to help you reduce your tax liability during retirement. But did you know that deferring your taxes can lead to greater growth in your portfolio? Take advantage of tax-deferred accounts like RRSPs. These accounts allow you to invest pretax dollars, meaning that they are more efficient in terms of gains over time.

With tax-deferred investing, your money grows faster, because you have more pretax dollars than you do post tax dollars. Put the money in before you pay taxes on it, and you have more to grow over time. This benefits you quite a bit in the long run and can result in a larger retirement nest egg.

CHAPTER TEN:

IT'S THE ECONOMY, STUPID!

Bill Clinton was right

During the 1992 presidential campaign, one of the rallying calls of the Bill Clinton campaign was "the economy, stupid," along with its variation, "It's the economy, stupid." Whether or not you think Bill Clinton was a good president of the United States, and whether or not you agree with his politics, the reality is that the economy really does impact your success in retirement, and economic changes over the last 150 years have resulted in the situation we see today.

As you prepare for retirement, and as you continue to manage your financial resources during retirement, it's important for you to understand some of the ways that the economic climate can influence your long-term prospects.

Fall of the gold standard

One of the ways that the money supply has been kept in check over time has been by backing currency with a precious metal, such as gold. At various times in history, currencies of major countries have been backed by gold or silver—and sometimes both at the same time.

The idea that something tangible and considered universally precious should form a "backing" for currency is one that occasionally surfaces, but has long since passed. The rise of central banks in major countries, and the weaning away from the gold standard, has created a greater money supply, and that means that inflation plays a greater role in our economy.

With the gold standard (and the silver standard), only so much money could be printed. A gold standard limits money supply even when the currency isn't 100 percent backed by the gold. During the Great Depression, for example, the United States couldn't print more currency because it required that the Federal Reserve have enough gold to back at least 40 percent of its notes.

After World War II, some of the leaders of the world's "major" countries met together at Bretton Woods. This conference established rules of international trade and monetary policy (and pegged exchange rates to the US dollar) and central banks could, if they wished, convert their dollar holdings to gold at a rate of thirty-five dollars per ounce. In some cases, countries (like France) made it a point to reduce dollar reserves in favor of gold to attempt to lessen the economic influence of the United States.

In 1971, President Richard Nixon announced that the dollar would no longer be converted to gold as done since Bretton Woods. Supposedly, the situation was meant to be temporary, and subsequent devaluations of the US dollar in relation to gold were made in anticipation of returning to something approaching the backing of international currencies with gold. By 1976, though, the farce was ended. All references to the definition of the US dollar in terms of gold were eliminated. Without the backing of gold, there was no need for other countries to convert their currencies to dollars before trading with other countries. During the 1970s, the foreign exchange market as we know it today began to manifest.

Now, most major currencies are "fiat" (translated, basically, as "let it be done" from Latin), which means that they are worth whatever the market says they are worth relative to other currencies. Additionally, governments, via central banks or other bodies, can increase the money supply at will, through a variety of economic and monetary policy measures, in order to achieve their goals.

As you can see, when you are required to limit the money supply, inflation is not as rampant. It's the increase in money supply, which provides more money in circulation, that encourages a faster rise in prices. If there is enough money circulating in the economy so that consumers can afford to pay more, then prices will rise. Right now, there really isn't much standing between policymakers and "printing" as much money as they want. In fact, thanks to the digital nature of our record keeping and the way our money is recorded, the formality of "printing" notes isn't even needed. All it needs is for someone at the central bank to announce that more assets are being bought from its own government, and the money supply is thereby increased.

Central banks and monetary policy

The point of central banks is to regulate monetary policy and oversee the supply of money. As a result, central banks also influence the economy. Monetary policy is the basis for economic policy.

As of this writing, the Bank of Canada is concerned because inflation is at 0.7 percent. The target inflation rate for the Bank of Canada is 2 percent per year, with an acceptable range of between 1 percent and 3 percent. The reason for this is due to the fact that policymakers think that 2 percent annual inflation presents modest economic growth that can keep things moving. At the same time, 2 percent inflation is considered moderate enough that consumers can easily keep pace with rising prices.

When an economy isn't growing enough, as measured by inflation and other factors, a central bank can take steps to stimulate growth. A central bank might cut the interest rate at which it lends money to other banks. This reduces the cost of money and can stimulate more borrowing. When more people can borrow, they tend to spend more. This drives the economy to increased performance. If interest-rate cuts designed to stimulate the flow of money through the economy aren't enough, the central bank can resort to quantitative easing, in which more money is created (let it be done) and injected into the economy.

All of these efforts are made in an attempt to get more money out there in the hopes that it will mean that consumers have the ability to pay for more goods and services. Once these things are in demand, then companies will have to hire more people to keep up with demand, and so those who have new jobs have money to spend, and the economy continues to grow.

Another impact monetary policy can have is on the stock market. In many cases, economic stimulus creates higher stock prices. Being able to borrow money at lower rates means better profit margins for companies, and that can mean improved confidence—and higher stock prices.

It's also worth noting that many policymakers (prodded by politicians who don't want to be caught with recessions on "their watch") consider it necessary to promote economic growth when down cycles come into being. The result is that, even though there might be market setbacks, the very nature of monetary policy efforts lead to stock market rebounds after downturns.

The risk associated with current monetary policies is that of more frequent and larger down periods. The idea that every down cycle has to be fought with efforts at stimulation is one that means that economy-cleansing periods of deflation are not permitted. As a result, some corrections might not be made. This constant striving for growth also means that there are likely to be, in the future, a greater number of larger economic events and stock market volatility. However, since it's a priority to keep propping up the system, recovery is likely to follow each event—at least in nominal terms.

This means that you need to plan your retirement investing strategy around the possibility that there could be several downturns during your retirement, and you need to be prepared to weather that so you can come out with your nest egg mostly intact (or at least capable of recovery).

Stocks as an inflationary hedge

Since inflation becomes a problem when economic growth is being stimulated, it's important to have access to assets that can beat inflation. Think about it: if you have a savings account that pays you 0.5 percent annually, but the inflation rate is 0.7 percent, you are actually *losing* money in real terms. You are losing 0.2 percent in purchasing power each year.

In many cases, due to the nature of our global monetary system, it's difficult for you to build wealth in real terms. Inflation is going to be a constant if things keep moving this way. You need a hedge against the ravages of inflation, and stocks can be that hedge. Even if your stock portfolio returns "only" 7 percent a year on average, you can do reasonably well. Even if inflation does hit that 3 percent a year mark, you are still earning 4 percent a year (before taxes and fees are considered).

If you are earning only 4 percent a year for your bond investments, that 3 percent inflation rate can be much more damaging, leaving you to earn 1 percent after inflation is factored in. Add in investment fees and taxes, and you are in real trouble.

Stocks can provide the hedge you need against inflation—and they can provide it without a great deal of expense and difficulty. If you rely on a managed portfolio, you might even be in better shape, since you know that, historically, stocks gain over time. Being able to count on these modest gains (gains that come without some of the risks accompanying other assets) can provide you peace of mind during difficult times. After all, if the policies of central banks are designed to stimulate economic growth and help the stock market get back on track, you will want to have stocks in your retirement portfolio.

Using stocks appropriately during the building phase of your portfolio can help you amass a large-enough nest egg that market events don't completely hinder your retirement. Choosing the right assets for your retirement portfolio can help you continue earning income later, even during a downturn.

And holding off on selling your stocks during market weakness can provide you with the means to enjoy better performance later, during the recovery.

Pay attention to cycles

Part of your planning is to pay attention to cycles. Don't think of an economic down cycle as permanent or extraordinary. Instead, consider that it's an opportunity to purchase some assets at a reduced price. The help of a knowledgeable retirement planner and investment professional can help you figure out a strategy that works for you.

During an economic down cycle, certain sectors perform well. Utilities tend to remain steady, and discount stores generally get something of a boost. This is because, even during tough times, people need the power to stay on. As they pinch their pennies, they turn to discount chains to help them save money in some areas of their budgets. However, the materials and consumer technology sectors tend to suffer during an economic down cycle.

You can use this knowledge to make decisions that can benefit your portfolio. As an economic cycle starts to go bad, you can sell technology stocks (or, if you have invested in a sector index, you can sell shares in that) before they bottom out. Use the money—from something you sold near a high—to purchase shares of discount stores or consumer products while these prices are still relatively low. Then, before the picture improves, you can buy shares of bottomed-out sectors and reap the capital appreciation as the stock market recovers.

This type of strategy requires that you pay attention, however. You can also use this method on a smaller scale by paying attention to business cycles. Trends related to shopping seasons (like Christmas and back-to-school) and real estate happen on a yearly basis, and you can use a little knowledge of these business cycles to help you make decisions about when it's a good time to buy and when it's a good time to sell.

If you don't have time to pay attention to these cycles, a good money manager can help you efficiently allocate your assets. A good investment adviser and planner can help you identify business and economic cycles and prepare you for the possibilities related to monetary policy.

CHAPTER ELEVEN:

STOCK VOLATILITY IN THE SHORT RUN

Don't panic

Part of avoiding panic during stock market down turns and times of volatility is the ability to understand what's happening. The right knowledge can provide you with confidence, even while everyone around you unloads his or her stocks—locking in losses—in a fit of panic.

It's important that you not panic in the face of stock volatility in the short run. First of all, if you have a solid investing plan that includes diversification through carefully chosen dividend-paying investments, you will likely be able to weather the current storm without too much trouble. Here are some things you should understand about stock markets, volatility, and the fact that the right assets can make a big difference over time.

Market sell offs of the past

There have been three major market sell offs in recent memory, those of the years 1987, 2002, and 2008. Each has sparked concern about the long-term viability of the stock market. However, each time, recovery has been relatively quick.

Crash of 1987

The crash of 1987 was known as Black Monday. In the days leading up to the big event, there was a great deal of volatility. The US economy had been slowing its recovery from the economic slowdown of the early 1980s, and the Dow Jones Industrial Average was rising, even as the economy experienced what was called a "soft landing."

Earlier in the year, in August, the Dow had reached the 2,722 level. However, the Dow was pulling back. Part of the run-up to the then-record was due, in part, to the rise of program trading. Technology had made an entrance into the world of trading, and computers were being used to execute many trades. With trading being done according to a program, and with the number of trades increasing as a result, it wasn't much of a surprise that records were being set.

However, with signs of economic slowdown, the Dow was pulling back (some said the markets were returning to normal). In October, the Dow began to exhibit more signs of volatility. It didn't help that the London markets were shut down for a severe storm and that Iran was firing missiles at US supertankers in the Middle East. US Treasury Secretary James Baker expressed his worry about the difficulties in the markets on Friday, October 16, giving investors an entire weekend to fret about what was happening.

STOCK VOLATILITY IN THE SHORT RUN

When markets opened in Hong Kong on Monday the nineteenth, the sell-off began. By the time US markets opened, on Black Monday, Asian and European markets had already lost quite a bit of value. The Dow itself lost more than five hundred points in a single day, accounting for 22.61 percent of its value.

Very few market crashes result from a single cause, and Black Monday was no exception. There were several causes blamed for the crash. At the time of the crash, there were international disputes about currency exchange rates, on top of geopolitical tensions in the Middle East. Also, the market was reacting to new concepts in arbitrage (related to index futures) and portfolio insurance issues. All of this combined to create a situation that meant a reduction of confidence in the markets. Many investors started unloading their stocks, and the result was a rolling crash around the world. Some say that the program trading exacerbated the problem once it got underway, while others insist that it was a big part of the initial problem—at least in the United States.

In any case, the crash shook the system up a little bit, but the recovery was relatively quick. Since the economy was still in a state of general recovery (even though expansion had slowed), things didn't remain down for long. Even though a group of economists predicted economic troubles to follow for a few years following Black Monday, things didn't quite turn out that way. In fact, the calendar 1987 was profitable overall. On January 2, 1987, the Dow opened at 1,897 points. Even though the Dow suffered a big setback in October 1987, it didn't change the overall positive tone of the year. When the Dow closed on December 31, 1987, it was at 1,939.

It's true that this was a far cry from the 2,722 level reached in August, and such a level wouldn't be seen again until 1989. But if you had invested in an index fund following the Dow at the end of 1986, and if you had managed to avoid panic selling following Black Monday, you would have ended the year ahead. If you had maintained your investments beyond that, you would have come out even further ahead as the market continued to climb.

Consider: even if you had sold your shares in an index at the lowest point of the Dow in the 2000s, you would still have come out ahead on the shares you bought prior to the crash of 1987.

Crash of 2000–2002

The market crash of 2002 had a much longer lead-up than the crash of 1987. In fact, according to a report from the Cleveland Federal Reserve, the crash of 2002 had been in the works since 2000. The crash of 2002 was the result of the bursting of the tech bubble as well as the result of a number of scandals—you probably remember the accounting scandals of Enron, WorldCom, and Arthur Anderson in the United States.

Not only that, but the tragic events of September 11, 2001, shook the very foundations of the economic system. The market was closed upon news of the attacks and was not reopened until more than a week later. The economy took a big hit at that point, and there were already signs of a slowdown in the works in any case.

There was a huge bull market in the run up to the crash of 2000–2002. Between 1987 and 1995, the Dow gained approximately 10 percent each year. Between 1995 and 2000, the Dow gained 15 percent a year. Gains of that nature were way out of line with historical trends. The entrance of more "regular" folks in the market, the explosion of the Internet and dot-com companies, and the fact that the generation of defined contribution plans was really hitting its stride all combined to create explosive growth for the stock market. This wasn't just the case in the United States, either. Markets around the world saw dramatic growth during this period.

A lot of factors combined to bring the Dow to a low point in 2002. But, even at its low point in October 2002 (notice how all of these events tend to happen in the autumn), at 7,286.27, the Dow was still much, much higher than it was prior to the crash of 1987.

The recovery process from the crash wasn't very lengthy, either. By this time, politicians and policymakers in the United States had become quite comfortable with the notion of intervening quite openly in ways designed to stimulate economic growth. Interest-rate cuts, policies (like tax cuts), and other strategies were used to boost the economy. And, of course, the recovery of the stock market was seen as the proof that such measures worked.

You can see from the chart below that market volatility was quite pronounced from 2000–2002, and you can also see that the recovery afterward was reasonably quick.

Dow Jones Industrial Average Index

Crash of 2008–2009

As much as we like to assign a single day to mark as *the* day that everything went wrong, stock market crashes don't happen that way. While there has to be the low point, the reality is that these crashes are usually seen coming at some point, since they are often preceded by a certain degree of volatility. Following the crash of 2002, the recovery began in earnest. Americans were encouraged to spend, and home ownership was encouraged.

Home ownership was encouraged to such a degree that "creative" financing methods were introduced. Interest-only loans, in which borrowers need only pay the interest for the first few years, were introduced. Low, low initial teaser rates were used to lure buyers into agreeing to bigger mortgages. Home values were rising, and so were prices, so bigger mortgages were needed to keep up. Also, many lenders had abandoned the old idea of a 20-percent down payment. Now, it was possible to buy a home with 0 percent down and a low teaser interest rate.

Because the economy was expanding at a nice clip, it seemed as though everyone was in good financial shape. Borrowers were told they could "afford" bigger homes and that with the increases in home values continuing, they would have no trouble refinancing their mortgages later, when the teaser rates ended.

On top of that, new financial derivatives were being structured. Securities based on mortgages were being created, sometimes mixing in subprime loans from less reliable borrowers with the better loans. Indeed, one of the reasons that so many lenders were willing to make risky loans was that they were just being sold off and repackaged anyway. The lender gets a fat kickback/commission, the borrower gets in a big house, and the investor makes lots of money on the high-rate returns that come with high-risk mortgages.

Everyone thought they could all get rich together. Everyone from politicians to bankers to consumers were comfortable with taking on risk.

However, soon major financial institutions began to fail. The fall of Lehman Brothers was one of the biggest shocks. The subprime loans and the credit default swaps (few of those investing in them even understood them) became too much. However, the United States wasn't the only country experiencing bank failures. Failures in Europe also came as a result of the global financial meltdown. In fact, the entire economy and currency of Iceland had to be completely overhauled.

Inklings of the mortgage crisis had first appeared in 2007. Even as the Dow reached a peak of 14,164 in October 2007, there were warnings about a possible bubble. In fact, by the end of 2007, legislation had been enacted in the United States that was meant to prop up the mortgage market to some degree. However, the situation kept deteriorating.

Beginning on October 6, 2008, the Dow closed lower for five consecutive sessions. The S&P 500 dropped, as did the Nasdaq. On October 24, 2008, a number of stock exchanges around the world experienced their worst drops in history. However, the Dow did not hit the low of this crash until March 2009, when it dropped to 6,469.

The aftermath

The US government was at great pains to stimulate the economy following such a devastating drop. It had been quite some time since the

Dow had been at such a low level. Why, even at its worst, the crash of 2000–2002 hadn't put the Dow below the 7,000 mark.

Economic stimulus in the form of tax rebates, tax cuts, interest cuts (even now the Fed Funds Rate is set at between 0 percent and 0.25 percent), and quantitative easing by the Federal Reserve's purchase of assets from the US Treasury and other sources was put into place. And now, a little more than six years after the meltdown really began in 2008, the Dow has more than doubled from its 2009 low.

Yahoo! Finance provides a chart that illustrates the lead-up to the crisis and the aftermath:

As you can see, the low point was actually during the first quarter of 2009. But by 2010, the Dow was solidly above the 10,000 mark. And, remember, that even at its worst in March 2009, the Dow still had a higher point than its level back in 1987.

Dow Jones Industrial Average Index

If you had started saving for retirement in 1986 and planned to stick with your plan for thirty years, you would still be ahead right now— very much ahead—just a couple of years before your retirement date. Stocks have had some shaking up in the interim, but they have gone on to recover. Even if you had had to sell low in 2009 for some reason, you would still have been ahead if you sold the shares you bought in 1986.

Market volatility

Market volatility is always present. On a day-to-day basis, the moves in stock prices can swing dramatically. However, it makes sense to step back and put this volatility into perspective—especially as it relates to long-term trends.

First of all, it is impractical to assume that any market will always end up ahead all the time. The nature of economies and markets is cyclical. There will always be downturns. You can look for the signs of a downturn by watching market volatility, since it always seems to pick up ahead of a crash. (You can even monitor the VIX, an index that follows market volatility.) It's also possible to pick up clues from technical analysis.

If you want long-term success, it makes sense to avoid trying to fiddle with market timing altogether. Instead, you can usually count on somewhat stable returns over the long haul if you include index funds and dividend-paying stocks.

It's always tempting to try and "time the market". Many people believe they can actually buy stocks at their lows and continually sell them at their highs. This can be done in theory only and "market-timers" almost always underperform the market in general. Remember it is "time in the market" that's important, not "timing the market". If you want long-term success and stable returns, hire a professional to manage a diversified portfolio of blue chip dividend paying equities, there is no better way to a rock solid retirement.

CHAPTER TWELVE:

CONCLUSION

Stocks as part of your Canadian retirement

The future is likely to hold more volatility as well as inflation. This makes it difficult to not only build wealth over time but also to avoid drawing down your nest egg too early. You are likely to live thirty, or even forty, years in retirement. You need to prepare for that ahead of time by building up your nest egg. The most effective way to build wealth over time is with the help of stocks.

Stocks can help you beat inflation in a way that fixed-income assets and bonds can't. Additionally, the current climate—and the likely climate of the future—means that having stocks in your retirement portfolio is also important. While you can include other asset classes in your retirement portfolio, it's vital that you include stocks. You also need to keep in mind the tax situation, since that can impact your overall returns as well.

CONCLUSION

Speaking with a retirement planning specialist can help you create a port-folio that works well for your situation, one that will make sure you don't outlive your money. The right investment manager can help you employ the right tax strategies and choose the right assets to help you meet your goals as a retiree.

The new Canadian retirement has a lot of potential, and you can reach yours with the right planning.

Chapter # 12: Conclusion

Rock-solid retirement: Five things to remember!

I've been guiding people to and through retirement for over thirty years. I've enjoyed this longevity because I think rationally and strictly follow some very specific guidelines. Here are some of the guidelines I've followed closely that have enabled me to help many people enjoy a secure, rock-solid retirement.

Five guidelines to retirement success:

1   Reduce the tax you pay

Do not pay one dime more in taxes than is necessary. When structuring your retirement plan, tax efficiency is the key. It's shocking to me that some people spend a lifetime saving for retirement yet put very little thought into drawing their retirement income in the most tax-effective manner. It takes time and expertise to draw up a retirement income plan that is tax effective. Take the time and speak with an expert in retirement income planning.

#2   Risk management is key

Firstly I've found that a lot of people fail to identify risk properly. Most believe the ups and downs of the stock market are their biggest risk. This, of course, is called volatility. But volatility is not the biggest risk to a secure retirement, not even close. The biggest risk is the possibility of outliving your retirement assets. Life expectancies are high and rising, and many retirements will last over forty years. Short-term volatility as a risk metric pales in comparison to the risk of outliving one's money. That's why a retirement plan must be meticulously structured to provide decades' worth of retirement income. This requires the assistance of a specialist; this is not the time to wing it!

#3   Beware the banks

The bank is an excellent place to get a loan, but not as a place to put your money. When you deposit money into a bank, you are really just providing them with the capital to lend to someone else. In turn the spread between what they pay you and what they lend your money out at turns into their profit. If you are going to deal with a bank from an investment perspective, it should be to actually buy shares in the bank and own a piece of this lucrative business.

#4   Forget market timing

When investing, it's time in the market, not timing the market. Timing the market is a fool's game and a retirement killer. No one can do this effectively, and anyone who says he can is lying. The only way to secure a long-term, financially stable retirement is to buy quality, adjust for particular sector weights, and let the dividends roll in, year after year.

#5   Hire a pro!

Very few people, regardless of background, are fully equipped to design, implement, adjust, and carry through with a full retirement income plan. The complexities of tax, investment, estate, and risk-management issues are enormous and ever changing, and you need an advisor who can guide you. Seek out the best, because this is no time for lost opportunity. Working with a retirement income specialist will allow you to enjoy your retirement with the peace of mind that your plan is sound and your relationship with your advisor will ensure it stays that way.

ABOUT THE AUTHOR

Brian Mercer is one of Canada's premier financial advisors. His practice, Mercer Private Counsel; focuses on providing advice to near and current retirees on tax effective income structures, succession planning and portfolio management strategies that are specific to those groups. He is a veteran radio show host on financial matters and seminar speaker focusing on retirement income planning.

To learn more, go to: www.mercerprivatecounsel.com

Made in the USA
Charleston, SC
16 October 2015